WHY

Discovering Your Essence is Important for a Life of Meaning

Carl Nafzger

Why: Discovering Your Essence is Important for a Life of Meaning

Notice of Rights

Notice of Liability

Hardback ISBN: 978-1-945464-03-4
Paperback ISBN: 978-1-945464-02-7
eBook ISBN: 978-1-945464-04-1

Published by:

Heritage Press Publications, LLC
PO Box 561
Collinsville, MS 39325

Terry 'n' Stacy

Enjoy

Thanks for your

friendship

Vaya Con Dios

Cecil 'n' Wanda

Nelson

CONTENTS

ACKNOWLEDGEMENTS

If I were to thank every person who played a role in guiding me along my path to success, the list of names would be longer than this book. As we go through life, we interact with so many people who influence the decisions we make and the directions we take. Very often, it is only years later that we realize how important a role someone played in our life. So while I cannot thank by name every person who has passed through my life, I want to say to them, "I am aware of how important you were to me and I appreciate the role you played in my journey to discovering my own essence and finding my path to success." There are, however, two people I must thank by name. One is my wife Wanda for her support and patience with my endless conversations about theology, philosophy and life in general. The other special acknowledgement goes to Lynndee Kemmet for her superb work ethic in making this book a reality.

FOREWORD

In June of 1987, I spoke at a racing conference held at Canterbury Downs in Minnesota. When I walked in, a trainer, Carl Nafzger was discussing the treatment of his employees—assistant trainers, exercise riders, grooms, hot-walkers and others. I was instantly impressed. I had worked with trainers for about 17 years and had met trainers who seemed to treat their help well, but I had not met one who had such a detailed, incentive-based program for employees.

I didn't meet Carl Nafzger that day, but I did meet him later in Louisville. In the 28 years since that first meeting, we have had many discussions about horse racing and training issues. Carl also worked with our equine program at the University of Louisville by accepting into his barn international horsemen from Southeast Asia as interns, by speaking at seminars or conferences we sponsored, by discussing management of employees in our College of Business classes and by discussing steward issues from a trainer's standpoint. In all that time, we rarely discussed Christianity. The first hint that his thoughts went far beyond his horses occurred when he loaned me Viktor Frankl's book *Man's Search for Meaning*. Then one Sunday, he spoke at our Episcopal Church about what Christ had meant to him and his wife Wanda. It was a pleasant surprise. I realized that while they never carried Christ on their sleeves, nor confronted us with Christianity, their Church or how we should lead our lives, they were, in their own daily lives, simply demonstrating what it meant to be a Christian.

Recently, Carl asked me if I would read and comment on a new book he was writing. His previous book, *Traits of a Winner*, focused on selecting, training and racing horses.

Hence, I expected, another book on training or some of his thoughts on current issues facing the racing industry. But after reading the first page, I knew that the book was on the joys and benefits of leading a Christian life. Specifically, how the word of God will provide each of us with messages that we need to hear in order to find our individual paths to success. A book on Christianity coming from a former professional bull rider and current horse trainer! It's not that those professionals are not in need of a little help from the Almighty, or are not aware of God. It was just that generally you don't expect one of them to write a book on that subject.

Consider the life of a professional bull rider. Rodeos are organized by towns, cities, counties, livestock shows and other organizations and managed by rodeo committees. They are often hundreds of miles apart. They may be sanctioned by the Professional Rodeo Cowboys Association, by other associations or not sanctioned at all. Bucking stock and other livestock are provided by stock contractors for a fee. Prize money comes from a pool contributed to by that rodeo, sponsorships, and cowboy entry fees. Cowboys compete to win, or come close. If they don't, they go home empty. This is not a circus. They are not paid to perform. They pay their own travel costs and if injured, their own medical bills. Always being on the road, and often injured, is part of this profession. Even if not bucked off, stepped on, or kicked, performing three, four or ten days consecutively takes a physical toll on even the best. And Carl was one of the best, and not planning to lose. It was a challenging, captivating way of life for a young man and it was a chance to make a good living. The top bull riders could earn in excess of $100,000 a year in today's dollars. Carl was from the West, as I was, where both cowboys and rodeo fans are in awe of champions. The expression that "If it had hair, he could ride it" was a real complement!

But Carl had other ideas too. And they came early. Once I asked John McBeth, a National Finals Rodeo Champion saddle bronc rider, if he was a contemporary of Carl. His response, "Sure, and let me tell you a story. We were at a rodeo on the East Coast, and the next rodeo we were headed for was at the Cow Palace in California. Before we got underway, a young bull rider (it was Carl) came up and asked if he could ride with us to California. I agreed but I told Carl he would have to drive at night. On that long trip, with Carl at the wheel, the car stopped and in the gray light of dawn all we saw were two columns with a "K" on each. To the "What the...?" Carl responded, something to the effect that, 'These are the Keeneland race track gates, and someday I'm going to race a horse here.'"

Carl's transition from bull riding is outlined in the book, but truthfully, becoming a trainer was like stepping from the frying pan into the fire! Racing too, for horsemen, is a game of winning or coming close. The track, taking a share of all wagers, plus other sources of revenue, puts up the purse money available for horses to win. Obviously, purse winnings go to the owners of those horses. For their efforts, trainers earn revenue by charging a daily fee for taking care of and training these horses – seven days a week! The daily fee is for the care of the horse and not much, if any, is left over. The trainer does earn 10 percent of any money won by a horse, which can be substantial. A winner's share of purses of $50,000 or $500,000 or more was certainly an incentive. If you are good at working with animals and can't wait to get to the barn in the morning, why not a career training horses? Being presented with a trophy by a Governor for a Classic win is also rewarding and a reflection of the God-given talents given to both you and your horses.

Trainers are often responsible for buying horses—often from breeders who are in the business of raising and selling younger horses at auction. And for even the knowledgeable horsemen, buying horses is like throwing dice! This is why experienced owners will often advise those who want to get into the game that "The last thing you need is a horse... The first thing you need is a trainer." With respect to horse owners, while younger trainers may have to accept horses from almost any owner, experienced trainers, who can train, who can win for owners, and who can get along with them, ultimately have a choice. Given Carl and his wife Wanda's racing record, and their Christian way in dealing with horses and people, they do have a choice. And they have selected well, as seen in their Derby and other innumerable 'big' wins. Their beliefs also contribute to their ability to handle the very highs and some of the extreme lows of racing that are experienced by both trainer and owner.

Obviously, being in the business of training requires management of revenues and expenses, compliance with track and other regulations, the selection, training and keeping of competent help, and as noted, developing a positive relationship with horse owners. Mentoring all employees is also part of the job. Carl himself had mentors like John Nerud. In turn, he also became a mentor to his long-time assistant Ian Wilkes. When Carl considered cutting back the number of horses he had in training, he suggested to many of his clients that they turn over their horses to Ian. Carl's desire to develop both horses and people is obvious to those who know him. His comments over the years, such as "surround yourself with people who want to be there" or "know and don't overwork your help" or "provide incentives," speak for themselves. Yes, there is camaraderie in the backstretch, but it is really a 'war.' Nevertheless, while

Carl and Wanda do everything they can to win, they do it the right way for horses, owner and their staff.

These comments are included here because there are no basic descriptions in this book of the framework of rodeo and racing in which Carl and Wanda have and are living their lives. What is in the book is an interesting, compelling and inspiring story about their lives with God and Christ as their guidepost. Their descriptions of Christianity, what it has meant to them, how it has affected their lives, the lessons they have learned and how that faith might improve the lives of others, are spelled out definitively and brought to life by personal examples.

Relying heavily on the Bible, considering its complexity, Carl does point out that our interpretation of Its messages differs. Each individual must find the meaning meant for him or her. Carl covers a wide range of subjects: finding yourself and a path that works for you, what God expects from us...and being true to yourself. His comments on success, independence, dreams, wants, failures, charity, mentoring, networking, depression and other life experiences that we all face are direct and to the point. This is a thought-provoking, practical, inspirational book that will point out a basis for success to those dissatisfied with their lives.

Educated by bulls, horses, people and life, Carl shares life lessons that are straightforward, profound, thought-provoking, and surpass those of many successful individuals in business, the professions or even in the academic or theological world that I have known. Consider these somewhat paraphrased examples:

- You will find who you are if you look inside yourself.

- No one is in your world but you.

- Whatever you don't want to quit doing reflects your passion.

- Bulls, horses and people will be good at what they are doing if that's what they enjoy and they have the capability to do it.

- Tribulations happen, but how you respond is in your control.

- Don't look for truth (about you) in the church, government or anywhere outside of God.

- So many people are afraid of failure they don't even try.

- Adversity is not punishment, it is guidance.

- If you learn from your mistakes, then you never fail—you only learn.

Think about the truth in each of these statements. For example, "No one is in your world but you" and remember the last time you were on a gurney headed for an operating table! Carl's Insight and examples are profound, simply stated and right on the money!

Readers will find that the book is spiritual and framed in a way that will both guide and *encourage* you. It is up to each individual to inwardly digest Carl's suggestions and then act, and accept responsibility for those actions. The book ends with an outline for a successful life, beginning with putting God first. Carl also suggests that if you bring Christ with you, you will find more than success at the end of your path. His emphasis, beginning to end, starts with working with God and taking responsibility. Even then success is not immediate—and for some, perhaps, a continuous search. I think Phillip Cary, author of *Good News for Anxious Christians,* would agree when he writes, "I don't think you just accept Christ once in your life, and then move on to figure out how to make real changes in your life...It's hearing the Gospel of Christ and receiving him in faith, over and over again, that makes real transformation." Carl and Wanda have heard that Gospel and are living examples of the effectiveness of that word, which is so refreshingly spelled out in this book.

Robert Lawrence, Ph.D., Professor Emeritus,
Equine Business, University of Louisville

PREFACE

I often tell people that I spent fifty-seven years writing this book. I was about fifteen when I started reading everything from the Bible to Steinbeck to Ayn Rand and a lot of other biographies that I hoped would help me figure out the meaning of life. Even after I became a professional bull rider, I read constantly while on the road traveling from rodeo to rodeo. This quest to understanding people and life started when, as a teenager, I looked around and saw so much hypocrisy in the world. The words and deeds of people didn't match up, and I did not understand how people could claim to believe one way and act the opposite. I grew up in a Christian community and even within that community, so often the actions of people were counter to the teachings of the Bible. Who I saw around me were not people who seemed happy and at peace, but rather people who were dissatisfied and frustrated with life. That so many people in my own Christian community seemed discontented led me to reject Christianity as a path for success and happiness. Once I rejected the Bible as the blueprint for a happy and successful life, I began searching for the path to success in other religions and philosophies.

Eventually, I found my way back to Christianity after realizing that the Bible really does have the answer for how each of us can find fulfillment, but my understanding of Christianity came to be something other than what I was taught as a youth. Christianity, I believe, is very individualistic. God really does care about every single one of us in a separate and unique way, and He uses His words to send each of us the messages that we need to hear in order to find our individual path to success. What I mean by this is important for understanding what I wish to impart to readers of this book. The understanding that I get from reading God's word in the Bible might not be the same as the understanding that anyone else gets from reading that same passage in the Bible. Two people reading one of Christ's parables might each take away something different from that story. Why? Because we gain from God's word what He knows we need from Him at that moment in our life. I do not believe that another person can tell you the exact meaning of a passage in the Bible. You must find in it the meaning *for you*. Some passages might not speak to you at all. Others might profoundly change your life. A Bible passage that had no meaning for you when you were twenty years old might have tons of meaning for you when you are sixty.

All of this became very clear to me in my own life as I aged. I could find no understanding of life in the words of Christ in my early twenties, but later in life, when I approached Christ's words with an open mind, I found tremendous meaning that put my life on a course to success. What I mean by having an open mind is that I stopped letting others tell me what Christ was saying to me and I opened my heart and mind to Christ and let Him speak to me directly. This individualistic view of Christianity might be counter to establishment, but it is my view of Christianity that is central to what I have to say in this book. I found that God had much to say to me once I accepted that I mattered enough to Him that He would speak to me directly.

I have come to understand that God has given us love, but love will die if we do not give it back. This book is my way of giving back the love God gave to me. My hope is that by sharing what I have learned through God's love, others will find their way back to God's love as well. It is in the presence of God that people can finally feel the peace and contentment that is the real mark of success in life. What you must do is open your heart and mind to God and let Him speak to you and guide you through His words and through the events that happen around you. How I learned to hear His words and let the events He caused in my life to guide me is the story I wish to share in this book.

Father, I pray that I will write the teachings of Christ that You have shown me. Please send the Holy Spirit to guide me and give me strength and wisdom to write Christ's teaching as I understand them and as they have applied to my life. Bless me to do Thy will, not mine. I ask this in the name of the Father, the Son, and the Holy Spirit. Amen.

Chapter 1

WE ARE MADE TO CREATE

Someone once asked me back in the 1990s what made me a success. I thought about it and at the time I didn't know the answer. In a way, it was the wrong question, because what the person really wanted to know was how my training techniques led to a Kentucky Derby win. The answer then and now is—I don't know. A better question might be simply—why did I win the Kentucky Derby? But the answer is still—I don't know. Wondering why you even bought this book? Don't worry, I do have answers.

The person who asked me how I became successful wanted a blueprint. They wanted me to tell them everything I'd done so they could copy it, but success doesn't work like that. There wasn't a set schedule of events that I had to follow to become successful—I did what I loved, and my life reflected the success of that choice. My point is that there is no one path for success, because all of our paths are destined to be different. You can't copy my actions, but you can copy my choice to do what you love.

When my wife Wanda and I started out as horse trainers, we didn't aim for the Kentucky Derby. It's always a fantasy in the back of your mind, but I came into horse training with the lessons I had learned as a bull rider. You can't think about what you have to go through to make it all the way to the Kentucky Derby, just as you can't think about what it takes to become a world champion bull rider. You just have to take each day one at a time and spend that day working at what you love. When I won the Kentucky Derby with Street Sense, some people asked me what I had been doing all those years between my Derby win with Unbridled in 1990 and my win with Street Sense in 2007. My answer was simply that I spent those years just doing what I do, which was training horses. Success in life is not about having a few big wins. It's about spending each day working at doing what you love. Reflecting back on my two Kentucky Derby wins, I think that two things played a part of those big wins in my life as a horse trainer. One was that I could not accept anything other than trying to succeed as a race horse trainer, but success didn't mean having one big win. It was about helping each horse achieve its potential and having consistent wins. When I had failures, I reflected on them, learned from them, and went forward. For example, I once took a good horse that loved to run and put him in a race in which he was overmatched. He was in the back of the pack with dirt flying into his face. He didn't like it, and what he learned from that experience was that he didn't like running after all. I made a mistake, but that mistake taught me to read my horses better and try not to put them in situations that could destroy their will to run.

The second thing that I believe played a role in my success in winning was that I also had faith that God was taking me where I was meant to go. If I was meant to win the Kentucky Derby, then I would do so as long as I kept trying and didn't sacrifice my principles for a victory. If I stayed true to myself and what I believed in as a trainer, and if a Derby win was meant to happen, it would. I knew that if I found the essence of who I was, then I would succeed with or without a Kentucky Derby win. Think about this—if God wanted to hide the most precious thing in the world, where would He hide it? You will find who you are if you look inside yourself. That essence holds all your talents and dreams, and once you tap them there is an unlimited potential of where God is taking you, even as far as the winner's circle at the Kentucky Derby.

As I said in the preface, I rejected God when I was younger, but the time I spent studying other religions and philosophies, combined with life experiences, gave me the perspective I needed to understand Christianity in a way that I could not as a teenager.

Because God is a creator, and we are made in His image, I believe that we are also meant to be creative. We are *meant* to build our own world (however small or large that world may be). Everyone has a path that can lead them to a life of fulfillment and success but the fact that we live in a world full of frustrated people is evidence that many people are not finding their path. They haven't determined who they are and what they really want to do with their lives. In other words, people are frustrated because they feel that their lives are unfulfilled and lack meaning. You must look for the meaning to *your* life and then you will find the meaning *of* life, because life is an individual journey. Until you find your own meaning, you will likely continue to feel frustrated and restless. It's no surprise that people who feel lost also often feel depressed and in despair. Until you gain the confidence to start living the life meant for you, you won't feel at peace with yourself. And the confidence to live *your* life will come if you can discover the essence of who you are. The path to a successful life is as simple as that—discover the essence of who you are and seek to live in harmony with your essence. I believe that the moment you start this journey to discover your essence, you will begin finding inner peace. This process of discovery is an exciting *LIFETIME* journey, not a quick trip, but it's a journey that will ultimately take you to the life that you will love to live.

What I have gained in the course of my life that made it possible to write this book now is perspective. Perspective was necessary to understand how all the knowledge from reading, the experiences, the events, and the people in my life interacted in ways that pushed my life along a path that led to success. In reflecting on my life training horses, I realized how much horses helped me understand that people must discover and live in harmony with their essence. Horses and people really aren't that different. Horses get just as depressed and distressed as people when they are asked to be something they are not, that is, to do something counter to their essence. If you ask a horse to do something counter to his essence, then you are asking him to do something of which he is not capable and that will frustrate him. I knew when I became a horse trainer that my approach to training would be very different from most other trainers. And, strangely enough, I best learned how to train horses by studying rodeo bulls.

In my rodeo career, I spent a lot of time observing bulls, and I learned the importance of understanding them in order to have success as a bull rider. This is one of my steps to success—take time to reflect on things and understand them. I would sit and watch bulls to see how each one moved when it bucked. Did it walk on its front feet, did the bull rear, was he flat or did he kick while he was spinning? All of these things would influence how I set my rope when I rode a particular bull and how I would position my body and program my mind. I do the same with horses and I think any good rider does. It's not how you ride horses or bulls, it's how you ride *this* horse or *this* bull. Each one is an individual. For example, if a bull walks on his front feet, you have to be real patient on him. A bull that drags his rear end and doesn't kick when he spins will slide you off your rope. You need to get more hold with your feet, hump over him more, and have a tighter rope. You have to keep up with him. If you are riding a bull that rears, you loosen your rope on him so that rope has some give. That will help you stay with that front end. Horses are like bulls. You have to figure out how to keep your balance with that particular horse and not interfere with that balance. It's about staying in harmony, and the only way you can figure that out is by studying the horse or bull you're going to ride. As a horse trainer, I did the same as I did with bulls—I observed them. Horses have their own way of running a race—some like to run inside, some outside, some like to run early. I'd figure this out and then tell my jockeys what each horse enjoyed. When you train horses you have to determine what they like the most and then build off of that. If you can come to understand each individual horse then you can figure out how to interact with each in a positive way. It seemed logical that if each horse had a different essence, then why not each person? When I saw how destructive it was to a horse when taken in a direction contrary to his essence, it seemed clear to me that the same would be true of people. It was those observations about horses that led me to wonder about the individual destinies of people, including myself. Could it be that we each have our own destiny, and that happiness and success would only come by discovering and fulfilling this destiny?

Just like each animal has a unique way of approaching his rider, people also have a unique way of approaching life. The way someone else does it just isn't going to fit, so you need to find the path that works for you. Also, just like I learned more with each bull and horse I studied, the more people you can interact with and watch, the more you can figure out how to interact with all people in a positive way.

Look for what people like most and build from that, and then take this same approach to events in your life. Remember, though, that these interactions, whether with bulls, horses, people, or events do not just impact us physically. Most often, interactions have mental and spiritual impacts on us. For example, I once competed on a bull in Oklahoma City named Tornado. He was one tough bull and he hadn't been ridden. An article came out in the press about what a great bull rider I was and that if anyone could ride this bull, it was probably me. I showed that article to a close friend of mine who was older and who had gained that thing called perspective and he said, "Too bad those bulls can't read." His point was that I shouldn't let that article influence my mental approach to riding that bull because things that influence us mentally can impact how we respond physically. I might have been successful on other bulls, but that didn't mean that I would be on Tornado—especially if I let myself assume that I would and didn't prepare. Spiritually, I also needed to make sure my pride didn't get in the way.

So as you can see, the path to success is three-fold: physical, mental, and spiritual. That's one of the things I loved about riding bulls—the union of all three parts. Once that chute opened, it was just me, the bull, and God. It was a feeling of complete independence because nothing outside of that mattered. Achieving that sort of independence has always been a spiritual quest for me, and is a part of my unique path to success.

Chapter 2

AN INDIVIDUAL PATH

As I said before, when I started my career as a horse trainer in 1971, I drew on the experience and knowledge I gained as a bull rider. I had to understand the horse the same way I had to understand the bull. What I wanted to understand was the essence of each individual horse. We so often hear people say, "That horse is destined to be a winner." Fine, but there's more to it than that. Then you have to ask, at what level could this horse be a winner? And in what event? I can tell you that if a horse isn't capable of being a race horse then no amount of training will make him a winner. It's the same with people. If you are not capable of being a great baseball player, then it's not likely that you will make the major leagues no matter how much you practice. However, that doesn't mean you can't live a life that involves baseball if that's your true love. If baseball is your love, then learn all you can about the game and keep your eyes open for those opportunities to be involved in it. There are many opportunities in the world of baseball other than playing on the field, but finding them requires being open to other possibilities. It also requires a willingness to work, just as the journey to discovering the life meant for you requires work. It is like hunting for a buried treasure. You can't find the treasure by sitting in a chair. You must get up and search! The only way to dig up that buried treasure is *to start digging* holes until you eventually find it. You will go through multiple jobs as you search for the life meant for you but every job, even the ones you hate, will teach you something. Through work you gain knowledge, self-discipline, and responsibility—all traits that are critical to success. It's through work that we discover more and more about who we are and what we want (or don't want) in our lives.

Work not only teaches us, it also gives us a sense of fulfillment and accomplishment in life. I know that many people dislike their jobs and that contributes to their frustration with life. Part of the problem in the work world is that people are led to believe that all they need is a particular education or training and they will have a great job and make good money and then they will be happy. But that old saying that "money can't buy happiness" is so very true. Human beings are creative by nature and much of the frustration we have with our jobs is that they don't allow us to express our unique essence. When you eventually discover your unique talents and skills and apply them to what you love, you'll find, or will create, the work meant for you. The jobs you go through in your life—the good ones and the bad ones—are all part of that process of discovering your talents and skills. If you don't go out and experience work, then you will never go through this process that could lead you to your dream job.

I used this approach toward work when I became a bull rider. I always had an affinity for animals and an ability to understand them. That's why my approach to bull riding and horse training was so focused on understanding the animals first. From the start, I knew that I wasn't just interested in riding a bull and staying on for eight seconds. My innate need to understand an animal led me to search for the essence of each bull. Some bulls are meant for rodeo and they enjoy the competition. Other bulls don't enjoy performing and traveling on the rodeo circuit and because of this, they don't have the heart for it. Bulls and horses, like people, will be good at what they're doing if it's what they enjoy and if it's something they have the capacity to do. This is why discovering your unique skills and talents are important. Attempting to be successful in an area where you lack the talent or skills for success leads to frustration. Jeff Copenhaver, a champion calf roper who has written the book series *God Wants You to Win!*, put it very well in his discussion of what he calls "just one more." According to Copenhaver, every one of us has something we love to do so much that we just don't want to quit. In Jeff's case it was that he'd be practicing roping and would tell himself that he'd rope just one more and then quit. Whatever it is that you don't want to quit doing reflects a passion and talent for something that God put inside of you. I agree with Jeff when he said that God wants you to follow that passion. He wants you to be a success.

When I was young and started riding bulls in high school, I felt a passion for bull riding. Later on, I felt the same way working with horses. In my search to understand the horse, I learned that success in training horses comes easy if you just let each horse be itself. That realization also taught me that success in life is much easier if you just be yourself. This is important for success—you must be yourself at all times in life. A big mistake many of us make in life is that we often think that something other than what we have now will make us the person we want to be. If only we had this job, or this much money, or that person to love, then we could become a better person. If you are waiting for a person, a job, money, or some other material object to make you a better person, then you will never feel successful and at peace. Become that better person now and that is the person you will take to the top of your own road to success.

When I was in high school, I had an algebra teacher named Robert Fisher. Some of us boys would go to his house and he'd try to give us some help with our algebra. I never did learn much about algebra but Mr. Fisher did teach me a lot about life. One of the most important things he said that I never forgot was that it doesn't matter what you do in life as long as you work to be the best that you can at it. It doesn't matter if you become a doctor, a mechanic, or a bull rider. What matters is that you focus on becoming the best doctor, the best mechanic, or the best bull rider that YOU can be. Mr. Fisher didn't say that we had to be the best in the world -only that we should become the best that we were capable of being, the best version of us.

To succeed at anything, at any level, you must give 110 percent. Simply put, you won't do that if you don't enjoy what you are doing.

Horses have talents and good trainers know how to use them. It's the same with people. A trainer's real job is to help a horse develop whatever capabilities the horse already has, and a good horse trainer has the ability to discover the essence of each horse and knows how to help that horse develop its talents so it can reach its full potential in whatever event it loves. Once you start discovering your true essence, fulfilling your destiny becomes an exciting journey. Once I discovered the essence of a horse, the training of that horse became very simple and it was exciting to see how far the horse would develop. Training is only complicated and hard work when you attempt to push the wrong horse into a career he's not meant to have. Horses are really quite simple. A horse will tell you what he likes and what he doesn't like. He'll tell you if he likes to race and at what level. He'll also tell you what strategy or style he most enjoys using in a race. Believe me when I say that horses do have their own strategies. The trainer's job is then very simple—manage the care of the horse in a way that keeps him healthy and happy so that he can perform at his maximum ability. The animal will take care of the rest. When I was getting close to Kentucky Derby day with Unbridled, I began to get nervous thinking about all the good trainers and horses we'd be up against. Then a friend of mine told me something very important, which was, "don't worry about the other horses because their trainers will mess them up. Just don't mess up your horse."

My friend's words stuck with me because they bring up an important part of the path to success—the spiritual side. A horse is happy in his spirit if he is doing what he loves. What breaks down a horse mentally and physically is pushing it to be what it was not capable of being. It's not much different with people.

In order to find happiness in life, we need to discover the unique talent that we've each been given. If you are in this situation in which you are living a life in contradiction to the life you want to live, then you must change it. Remember, people have free will and that means that you can choose to take control of your life. You have the freedom to discover yourself and live your destiny. If you are not living the life meant for you, then YOU have let yourself down. You need to find yourself and then make the choices that fit who you are. You won't find real success trying to be something that you are not because you will be acting counter to your essence and that leads to inner turmoil, not inner peace.

God has given to each of us talents that we can use for success. And by talents, I mean skills, not the often-used Biblical definition of talents meaning money. The parable of the faithful servant in Matthew shows that God expects us to use the abilities He has given us, and when we do, we succeed. Matthew 25:14-29 says:

For the kingdom of heaven is as a man traveling into a far country, who called his own servants, and delivered unto them his goods.

And unto one he gave five talents, to another two, and to another one; to every man according to his several ability; and straightway took his journey.

Then he that had received five talents went and traded with the same, and made them other five talents.

And likewise he that had received two, he also gained other two.

But he that had received one went and dug in the earth, and hid his lord's money.

After a long time the lord of those servants cometh, and reckoneth with them.

And so he that had received five talents came and brought other five talents, saying, 'Lord thou delivered unto me five talents: behold, I have gained beside them five talents more.'

His lord said unto him, 'Well done, thou good and faithful servant: thou hast been faithful over a few things, I will make thee ruler over many things: enter thou into the joy of thy lord.'

He also that had received two talents came and said, 'Lord, thou delivered unto me two talents: behold, I have gained two other talents beside them.'

His lord said unto him, 'Well done, good and faithful servant; thou hast been faithful over a few things, I will make thee ruler over many things: enter thou into the joy of thy lord.'

Then he which had received the one talent came and said, 'Lord, I knew thee that thou art a hard man, reaping where thou hast not sown, and gathering where thou hast not strewed.

And I was afraid, and went and hid thy talent in the earth: lo, there thou that that is thine.'

His lord answered and said unto him, 'Thou wicked and slothful servant, thou knewest that I reap where I sowed not, and gather where I have not strewed.

Thou oughtest therefore to have put my money to the exchangers, and then at my coming I should have received mine own with usury.

Take therefore the talent from him, and give it unto him which hath ten talents.

For unto every one that hath shall be given, and he shall have abundance: but from him that hath not shall be taken away even that which he hath.'

This parable in Matthew made me understand that we must use what God has given us. Each of us has unique talents and skills and success in life comes from discovering what those are and nurturing them. It doesn't matter if you have a multitude of talents or only one. God has given you something that you can use to find success in life but *you must find it* and use it. You must heed the advice of Christ to build on and use those talents. Our talents are tools given by God so that we can live a successful life. If we waste our talents, we not only waste God's gift, we also waste our life.

Chapter 3

DO WHAT YOU LOVE

So how do we go about using our skills to the best of our ability? It has often been said that success in life comes from doing what you love. This is really true because success is nothing more than living the life you were meant to live. A horse that really loves to race will put out 110%, 100% of the time because he is doing what he wants—running. If you are doing what you truly love, then you won't quit even when everything seems to go wrong. There were times in my rodeo career that it seemed no matter what, I just couldn't stay on the bull. And there have been times during my career as a horse trainer when it seemed I just couldn't win a race. But whether winning or losing, I still enjoyed my life. Although, I'll be honest, winning was more fun. If you are doing what you think you love but are not happy, then the first thing you must understand is the difference between truth and deceit.

Being truthful means that you are honest with yourself about what you need in your life and what you love. Deceit is pretending to be what you are not and trying to build your life on that deceit. Sometimes what you think you want in life isn't what you really love and what you are meant to be. Far too often, we deceive ourselves into thinking that we are living the lives we really want and doing the things we love when we are not.

I will give you an example. Many years ago, Wanda and I wanted to buy this 160-acre ranch, and we had dreams of how to build that old piece of property into what we wanted. But when we got enough money to buy it, we didn't want it anymore. I asked myself, why? And then I realized that what that place meant for us wasn't actually that ranch, but the sense of independence that ranch would bring. So then we started figuring out what would give us what we needed. A nice house and place takes money, but then you also have to take care of it and you need money for that. So then I started reflecting on what independence really is and I realized that it was simply being in control of self. Independence was connected to controlling my own destiny and when I look back on my life, I realize that this has been a pattern of my life.

For me, independence has been a driving force in my life. I grew up on a ranch, but I didn't want to work for a rancher because then I wouldn't be independent. I had a lot of offers for different jobs including being a rodeo judge, a stock manager, or a chute boss. None of them really interested me. Independence is the freedom to do what you really love and to control your own life. For me, these jobs would not give me the independence that I wanted. I did work on a ranch (Polo Ranch) at one point, but on my own terms. It proved to be a good move because that's where I was introduced to working with Thoroughbreds. It's also where I began to build a network of people who have played important roles in my life over the years (we'll talk more about networks later). Although I was offered a full-time position at the ranch, I created a different agreement. I worked part-time so that I could continue to ride bulls as I was easing out of my bull riding career and starting to move in another direction. I needed to keep riding the bulls for my income, but I was in a stage of figuring out my next move in life. I kept my freedom to rodeo and earn income at the same time that I got some work that gave me experience training Thoroughbreds. That work also helped start me down the path of my next phase in life—training race horses. In return, the ranch got an extra employee who could fill in and help break horses but without the cost of supporting me full-time. That job at the ranch gave me another benefit, years later. The daughter of the couple who owned the ranch—Mr. and Mrs. John Morris—married a national sportscaster who, years later, was covering horse racing. He interviewed me and gave me national television exposure, partly because of our personal connection. A past connection gained me some public exposure that helped make me more known as a horse trainer. I don't believe in coincidence, and I know that by being true to what I needed, the dominoes of my life started to line up.

So how do you know what you need in life for success? Start by being quiet and have faith in the invisible. This is an important point. There is that old saying that "seeing is believing." Unfortunately, too many of us only believe what is visible to us. Yet, what is invisible is most important—"While we look not at the things which are seen, but at the things which are not seen: for the things which are seen are temporal; but the things which are not seen are eternal" (2 Corinthians 4:18). It has always bothered me that so many people will not accept anything without proof. First, what one person accepts as proof might not be accepted by another. But more importantly, the constant need for proof shows just how many seem to lack faith—in anything. It isn't just a loss of faith in God that we see in our society. People have also lost faith in their ability to take responsibility for their lives and do what they love. At some point, you are ready to take a leap of faith and believe that you can live the life meant for you to live. *My life hasn't proven the Bible correct. The Bible has proven itself to me.* You can see the proof of the words of Christ not just in my life, but the lives of many others. Have some faith in the Bible and I guarantee that in time, it will prove the truth of its words to you. I agree with a comment that I once heard: "Even if the Bible is a lie, it's still the only way I'd want to live my life." But if you doubt the Bible's truth and teaching, then put it to the test. Live by it and see what happens.

What you need to hear and feel is inside of you, not outside of you. When you feel, you tap into the eternal power and wisdom of God. The way to determine what you really need in your life is to *feel* it. What you *think* you want is often not what you really need for your happiness and success in life, but rather something you think is the way to get what you want. Keep in mind that what you need is not necessarily something tangible, like a material object. For me, it was independence. Others might have a need to create art or music or even create a business from the ground up in order to feel fulfilled. Some might have a need to work with the poor because they have a need to feel that they are making a difference in the lives of less advantaged people. And yet others might need the security of working for someone else. Pursue what you need in life and it will guide you toward your purpose in life and to what will make you happy.

I want to stress here that this journey of life is a continuous one. You don't wake up one day and reach the end of this journey. If you wake up, then you are alive and therefore still on the journey. I am in my seventies and still on my journey, but I have already succeeded in having two careers—bull riding and horse training—which I have loved. During both of those careers, I spent each day doing what I loved and, in the process, earned financial rewards and recognition that landed me in the National Museum of Racing and Hall of Fame, The PBR Ring of Honor, and the Texas Rodeo Cowboy Hall of Fame. But my journey in life hasn't ended because I've found success doing what I love. Being a bull rider and a horse trainer has simply been part of the journey toward finding my real essence. Bulls and horses have been some of my best teachers in life. Working with both has helped me see my inner truth of who I am. But, I am still on the journey of discovering what God really meant for me to do in this life. I am still on the path toward achieving that which I was predestined to do in my life that contributes to the glorification of God. In other words, I am still working to discover and fulfill my role in God's larger plan. My inner peace comes from the fact that I am doing what I love and feel at peace and that tells me that I am at least on the right path toward the ultimate destiny given me by God.

You start this process by discovering the truth of who you are and what you love to do. When you do that, all of a sudden, you will feel free and at that moment, you can start on *your* path to fulfill your destiny. It will not be a smooth road if lessons are to be learned, but it will be the right road for you.

Thoreau said it best in *Walden* when he asked the question of who owns whom? Do you own the house or does the house own you? That question stuck with me as far back as my days in rodeo. If your dream is to live in a gorgeous house and use your home as the catalyst to build a beautiful neighborhood around you for all who live there—if that is your dream—then fine. But, if you just want a gorgeous home to show off, then you might find yourself a slave to it and you will not have time to pursue your real destiny in life. Again, it goes back to my warning that you must be sure what you are pursuing in life are your dreams and not just wants.

Everything leads back to acceptance of who you are. It is learning to love what God has made you. God has made you what you are so you should love who you are. Accepting what God made you makes it possible for you to love yourself and then you can accept and love your neighbor. You can love them for what they are—God's creation.

Chapter 4

ON DISCOVERING WHAT YOU LOVE

Discovering what you would really love to do with your life is a life-long journey that is usually full of adversity. You have to accept that everything is a learning lesson that is guiding you to your destiny. One problem for so many people is that they want to do too many things. You notice this when people say things like, "I love this and I love that and I love this" and on and on. Jumping from one love to another is part of growing up, but people also take on too much. Sometimes multiple commitments can't be helped. We all have commitments we've made to family, to friends, and to our jobs, but you need to remember to love yourself so that even while you work to fulfill these commitments, you don't stop searching for the essence of who you are, given to you by the One who made you.

The recognition that God created you allows you to love yourself, and once this happens you can begin to see the destiny He has placed within you. When you begin to love God's creation of you, then you will come to realize the importance of taking the time to study Christ's teachings in order to search for the essence of yourself. Once you have discovered that essence, you start on the path of learning everything you can about what you want or need. When the time is right, the doors will open for you.

Once Wanda and I made the decision to commit to a new
direction in life, we set about pursuing a means to get there.
One day I called Wanda at school (she was still teaching
then) and said, "Wanda, can you get away and we'll go
eat lunch?" She agreed and we took a few moments to eat
together. While at lunch I told her that I'd figured it all out.
We had studied it and we had researched it and I said, "I'm
ready to train horses." I told Wanda my plan and she agreed
to it. She resigned from teaching and we went to Texas,
where she did some teaching while we started on the road
to become horse trainers.

Our first decade as horse trainers was filled with many
disappointments, but it was a learning phase for us. And
most importantly, we were happy because we were doing
what we loved and were on the path to building our
dream. In time, we took the next leap, and Wanda stopped
teaching completely. We put our bags in a hatchback Vega
and headed further down the road. Funny, it seems that all
the old-timers in the horse racing world then had a Vega of
some sort.

I wasn't a fresh-faced eighteen-year-old kid out of high
school when I made the decision to start down a new path
doing what I loved, and it didn't matter. It is never too late
to start on this process of self-awareness in order to find your
destiny. If you've been married twenty or thirty years and
the kids are grown and you and your spouse realize that you
want to be farmers, then do it. The wants that you pursued
early in life got you where you are now and that is not always
a bad thing. You learn from where you have been and
where you are now. You don't ignore what's happened in
your life because it's all valuable. The family, the friends, the
love you have built in your life along the way are all good
and they are all forms of success if the others you have

touched have gained from you and you from them. If you put your family first in the earlier stages of your life, then you and your family both won because you're a good spouse and parent who educated your children and set them on their own path for a successful life.

What I'm trying to say is to be positive about what you have accomplished in life and don't live off past regrets. Go forward! Forward is always an option. Maybe you are thinking, "If I could have just been the race car driver I wanted to be, I would be happy. Now I'm too old." You need to let it go and count your blessings from where you are. The idea of being a race car driver might have been a want rather than your destiny, anyway. What you need to do at this point in life is go inside yourself and discover your essence and your destiny, and put the rest of your life on the path toward it. As the Scriptures say, "Seek and ye shall find, knock and it shall open" (Matthew 7:7). Look inside yourself and the door with the answers will open.

Here is my advice for doing what you love: take what you think you love and just start doing it. It's as simple as that. That's how I got into bull riding. It's a bit of a funny story. I went to my first bull riding competition at sixteen. I took a girl on a date and we went to watch a guy from our class ride. I left there thinking that you had to be an idiot to ride bulls, but the girls sure seemed to like bull riders. I ended up talking to a guy in class about riding bulls as we hatched a plan. My dad had feeder bulls and we talked him into letting us build a bucking chute—if he could put me on my first bull. So we built a chute and some classmates and I gathered some of my dad's bulls in a pen and started riding them. I rode that first bull about three jumps. But while I might not have lasted long on that first bull, I was hooked on bull riding! When I graduated in 1959, I joined the rodeo team in college. Every

Wednesday and Sunday, we'd go down to where they'd do bull try-outs and we'd get on the bulls to test them out for the rodeos.

Eventually I turned professional, and I headed on down the road with a few pairs of Levi jeans to join the professional rodeo circuit. Honestly, it was a bit like running off to join the circus, but the point is that if you think you'd love to do something, you just do it. Once you get started, you just keep learning. As you learn, you keep breaking through to the next plain. These plains keep coming at you and that's the excitement of the journey of life. You just keep moving from plain to plain and advancing in life.

Not everything we try in life ends up taking us into a successful career, but everything teaches us more about ourselves. Even attempts that go badly can lead to good things if we pick ourselves up and learn. I had a childhood friend whose son wanted to be a rock singer so he ran off to California at fifteen. Well, along the way in his rock singing career, he fell into despair and hit bottom. But rather than letting his mistakes defeat him, he learned from them. He went back to school, then on to college, and today he's a medical doctor living in San Antonio, Texas. The point is, trying something and then discovering that it's not for you isn't failing, it's learning. You can make mistakes, seek forgiveness, and move forward again. God won't abandon you, He'll help you. If you can believe this—and you should—this will give you the courage to try and find the life meant for you.

My own experience of this sort of scenario is with young people who, like me, wanted to be a rodeo bull rider. The life of a rodeo bull rider can be great if you really want to be one, as long as you don't mind getting on the bulls and can accept the injuries and pain and the traveling. But I knew lots of young men who wanted to be bull riders until the injuries piled up, and then they decided they didn't want to be a bull rider after all. And that's fine, because you can't figure out what you really love and want to do with your life unless you try what you think you love and see if it works for you! If you truly love something, then adversity becomes a learning lesson as you continue to move forward.

Consider this—if you inherit ten million dollars and never had a penny before, then you'll think you are rich. But in this world, ten million dollars can be gone in an instant. Think of how many people won a big lottery and were broke in just a few years. Now, consider the person who neither inherits nor wins that money, but rather earns it. Well, along the way of earning it, that person not only learned the value of money but also about taxes, savings, and other money management issues. The point here is that we learn through hard work and through adversity, and those lessons can help us appreciate what we receive. Things that come too easily are neither appreciated nor lasting.

For the young people reading this book, I say to you that this is the luxury of being young. Youth is that time of life when you can more easily try different paths in life in pursuit of the life you really would love. Older readers, however, probably have already learned many lessons. If you are older, then look for those lessons from your life and reflect on them. You have the advantage of having at your fingertips lessons that can help you find the essence of who you are and the life that matches it. What you need to do is pull up those lessons, reflect on them, and let them guide you forward. If you are working hard but nothing seems to be coming to you, wait and have faith.

Christ is hope and faith. Remember the words of Christ—faith even the size of a mustard seed can move mountains—"Truly I tell you, if you have faith as small as a mustard seed, you can say to this mountain, 'Move from here to there,' and it will move. Nothing will be impossible for you" (Matthew 17:20). I will say it again. Success is the fulfillment of who you really are, but getting there will be a life-long journey. It is also a journey with many twists and turns because what you want from life in your twenties isn't the same as what you think you want in your forties, your sixties, or even your eighties. That is the difference with wants—they change over time. Dreams really don't. Success is about becoming who you really are and learning to separate your needs, or your dreams, from your wants.

Chapter 5

BEWARE OF STRESS

Separating your needs from your wants is essential to your journey for success, because trying to attain what isn't meant for you does nothing but create dissatisfaction and stress. And stress should be avoided at all costs. As the Bible says, *"Take therefore no thought for the morrow; for the morrow shall take thought for the things of itself"* (Matthew 6:34)

I must emphasize this point—stress, both physical and mental, can destroy our lives. But the funny thing is that we are often the creators of that stress! We are literally making the thing that could destroy us. I've often said that stress is one of the most destructive things for a race horse. It comes from mental pressure on the horse or from physical injuries. However it comes, once a horse is stressed, the immune system is destroyed. Once that happens, it usually spells the end for the horse. It works the same way with people. Living a life that is contrary to our individual essence creates stress, which can destroy our mental, spiritual, and physical health. It's like forcing a work horse to be a race horse when what he really wants is to spend his days on the farm pulling the plow. On the farm he is happy and at peace. On the race track he is stressed and depressed. Eventually, it destroys him.

Not every horse is meant to be a star on the race track or in the show ring, and there's nothing wrong with that. Is the job of a plow horse less important? Well, it's the same with people. It doesn't matter what earthly career you choose. Through God's grace and forgiveness and guidance from Christ's teachings, you have the freedom to discover your essence and pursue whatever career makes you feel happy and at peace in your life. If you do that, then you will not only be a success, but in achieving that success your life will be a reflection of the glory of God.

This focus on a stress-free life is dominant in so many philosophies and religions, including Christianity. But the unique beauty of Christianity is the emphasis on forgiveness. Christianity teaches that by the grace of God through Christ's death, we have been saved. The importance of this is that Christ's death took away the burden of our sins, which means that all of us start with a clean slate. Christianity is really quite simple. God has placed within each of us our unique skills and talents that will allow us to find success in our lives. We have the free will to take the actions needed to discover our inner essence and pursue our destiny. We also have the freedom to make mistakes along the way—mistakes are how we learn. And all we must do to get back on our path to success is acknowledge our mistakes and seek forgiveness—repentance—and accept that forgiveness. It is interesting to me that so many people can't seem to accept God's forgiveness. They spend years of their lives punishing themselves for their mistakes rather than moving on with their lives. In truth, God has given us, through grace, the free will to choose to pursue our destinies, make mistakes, seek forgiveness, pick ourselves up, and go on to success. All we have to do is believe in God so that we can believe in ourselves and take that leap of faith required to follow our destiny. If we go off track, we simply must repent and learn, and then watch for those signs from God that will guide us back to our path to success.

It really is as simple as that, but even I will admit I had many times in my own life when I rejected Christ. As I said earlier, I was still a teenager when the hypocrisy I saw in people who claimed to be Christian caused me to reject Christianity. I later realized that I was wrongly blaming Christianity rather than the individuals. But I found my way back to Christianity because in the end, I realized that the teachings I found in other religions or philosophies were already covered by Christ. There is nothing in life that Christ didn't address in his teachings. Some might disagree with this, but I believe that Christianity is very individualistic. Why are there so many variations of Christianity and so many theological debates on the meaning of the Bible? Because the Bible speaks to each individual differently and not every word in the Bible has the same meaning or approach for everyone—but the truth is consonant (meaning that it is always in agreement or accord). Some verses have a powerful impact on one person and no impact on another. What you take away from the Bible depends on what guidance you need at the time. If you approach the Bible with an open mind rather than interpreting it as others have told you to do so, you might be surprised at how much Christ's words speak directly to you. You will hear the words you are meant to hear at any given time. There are many different Christs—the loving Christ, the forgiving Christ, the teaching Christ, the suffering Christ, the enforcing Christ, ETC. All of them are one in Christ. The one that speaks to you at any moment in your life will depend on the one you need at the moment.

I can't say this enough: in the words of Christ, you can find guidance on how to discover what you are meant to be in this life and how to achieve that destiny. But remember that Christ's words speak to each of us as individuals. What I gain from Christ's teachings might not be the same as what you get. We are each on different paths in life, so don't let Christ's words be interpreted for you. Let Christ speak to you through a friend, a minister, a psychiatrist, a stranger, or through events. If you are uncertain if the words you are hearing are true words from Christ, then test them against the Ten Commandments. In other words, simply ask yourself if what you think you heard violates any of the Commandments.

In my own life, I have found meanings within Christ's teachings that have helped me find the right path in life for me. I believe that you, reader, can also find the truth of who YOU are. The meaning of your life is inside you but you must discover it—"If you continue in my word, *then* are ye my disciples indeed. And you shall know the truth and the truth shall make you free" (John 8:31-32). It's a sad fact of life that the saying "most people live their lives in quiet desperation" even exists. So imagine a world in which the majority of people are not living in quiet despair, but in the full understanding of who they were meant to be.

I admit that what I have to say in this book isn't necessarily original. There are so many before me who have written books aimed at helping people find themselves and get on the path to a successful life. In fact, I've read many of those books and many of them have contributed to helping me find my way in life. Yet, despite all these books full of excellent advice, the world is still full of people who are searching for a better life. Why is that? Many of the same books I've read have made the bestseller lists, so obviously people are buying them. Are they turning into paperweights instead of being read? Do people read them and just not understand the message? Or, do people understand the message but simply choose not to listen? Whatever the reason, many people are still living those lives of quiet despair, and my hope is that what I have learned through my own life will help some of you who are still searching for your life's meaning. You must, however, begin that search if you are ever to find success in life. You must be open to change if you expect a change in your life! Think of the advice from Matthew 13:4-8. As the Parable of the Sower says, you can be the solid ground from which good seeds bring forth fruit.

And when he sowed, some seeds fell by the way side, and the fowls came and devoured them up:

Some fell upon stony places, where they had not much earth: and forthwith they sprung up, because they had no deepness of earth;

And when the sun was up, they were scorched; and because they had no root, they withered away.

And some fell among thorns; and the thorns sprung up, and choked them:

But other fell into good ground, and brought forth fruit, some a hundredfold, some sixtyfold, some thirtyfold. (Matthew 13:4-8)

If you are questioning your life, then you are already on your path to success. Questions are good, though I often wonder if I drove my parents crazy with all of mine! From my earliest memories, I was questioning everything in life, and I had a tendency to reject what I didn't consider a satisfactory answer. One of the other reasons I turned away from Christianity when I was a young man was because I turned away from people who I felt could not understand my life. I was a cowboy...what did the preacher really know about me? Today they have cowboy church on the rodeo circuit, but there was nothing like that during my bull riding days. I didn't know any ministers who had ridden bulls or traveled the rodeo circuit so I figured, who were they to give me advice about my life? Some of you might wonder how I can offer advice on life to readers whose lives are probably quite different from mine. Thankfully, I have learned in my life what I wish I had known as a young man—that good advice can come from many directions. As I grew older, I learned that those ministers of my youth, the ones I ignored because they'd never even sat on a bull, actually had some good advice. Too bad I just wasn't ready to listen at that time and turned away from the Good News they were trying to share with me. Thankfully, my uncle's prediction came true. Even as I turned my back on Christ, my uncle told me that in the course of my life, I would prove the truth of the Bible verse that after one tries all other things, one will realize that as Christ said, "I am the way, the truth and the life" (John 14:6). It took a lot of years, but my uncle ended up being right.

If people only listen to those to whom they can relate, then perhaps what I have to say here isn't meant for everyone. Perhaps what I have to say will only be heard by those who feel they can relate to my life experiences and I to their life. I don't know how many people will read this book and maybe fewer still who will follow the advice. But if it can help one person change his or her life, and that one person then helps another, and so on, then the book will fulfill the goal I set when writing it. I would like to think this book is like a rock thrown into a pond. It's just one rock, but the ripples just keep spreading all the way to the shore, touching everything in the pond. Our lives can be like that. We can live our lives in a way that sends positive ripples throughout the whole pond, and that, to me, is the definition of success.

Chapter 6

UNDERSTANDING TRUE SUCCESS

Earlier I mentioned that the first step to success was avoiding stress. The second one is to know what true success really is.

But seek ye first the kingdom of God, and his righteousness; and all these things shall be added unto you. (Matthew 6:33)

There are two books I read in my early twenties that began to impact my thinking. One was *Psycho-Cybernetics* by Maxwell Maltz and the other was *Think and Grow Rich* by Napolean Hill. At the time I purchased these books in my early twenties, my attitude was so bad that I figured that on the last page the author would say, "I sold you this book now you figure out what gimmick you can do to make a lot of money." This was a period in my life where I had turned my back on Christianity and my view of everything in life was very negative. Because of my own attitude, what I didn't understand about the books was that they had been written in a positive form to help, not hinder.

I came away from reading Psycho-Cybernetics with a new understanding of the verse in Genesis 1:27 that tells us that God created man in His own image. It began to occur to me that if God created us in His own image then He must have also given us all the knowledge we need to discover and be who we are. Think and Grow Rich made me understand and accept the concept of responsibility of self—it doesn't matter if your father was a drunk or your mother was a prostitute, once you are the age of understanding, your life is up to you. I came away from that book accepting that I am responsible for my life and I had to accept the responsibilities of self. At that time in my life, I thought what I wanted was money. Having money is no longer the goal of my life, but what I accepted at that time was that if I wanted money, it was up to me to figure out how to get it. What I hadn't yet learned at the time was the difference between money and wealth, and between wealth and success.

The first mistake most of us make in life is that we fail to understand success. Most people define success in terms of wealth and from there they equate money with success. The truth is that many wealthy people are unsuccessful in other parts of their lives, while many less wealthy people actually live very successfully. So while wealth might be a part of how one defines success, it is not in itself success. However, that is not to say that wealth is a bad thing. Throughout history, many have interpreted Christ's teachings to imply that wealth is sin and poverty a blessing. I disagree with this interpretation.

Take this from Christ's teachings:

> *And the disciples were astonished at his words. But Jesus answereth them again and sayeth to them, "Children, how hard is it for them that TRUST in riches to enter into the kingdom of God! It is easier for a camel to go through the eye of a needle than for a rich man to enter into the kingdom of God." (Mark 10:24-25). "With men it is impossible, but not with God: for with God all things are possible. (Mark 10:27).*

To some, this might sound like Christ is saying that you cannot be financially well off and also be a follower of Christ. However, if this is true, then why are some of the greatest people in the Bible also some of the most wealthy? What about King Solomon, the wealthiest and wisest king of the Bible? What about the wealth of Job or of Abraham? With these people in mind, people favored by God, I would argue that God is less concerned with our wealth and more concerned by our reaction to it.

Wealth itself is not wrong, but the deceitful sense of power that you can get from it and misusing it can be. So let's think for a moment. Why do we care about wealth at all? Well, that's easy. Wealth allows us to have things, right? We earn money and trade it for things that we think are valuable to us. So if you think of it like that, the only true worth of money is what you're willing to exchange it for. You have control over how you use wealth, just as you have control over everything else in your life. If you do not let money deceive you and you do not make it an item of worship, then under God's guidance it can be a blessing that can establish your kingdom on earth as well as heaven. Wealth allows you to care for your family; it allows you to support other people on the road to their dreams; it can be used charitably to help people having a hard time; it can be used to support other worthy ministries. Overall, wealth can be a sign of God's blessing as you focus on the path He has laid out for you. The key to understanding the usefulness of wealth is that you cannot be deceived into believing the money belongs to you. It belongs to God.

Over the years, wealth has taken on a wider definition for me than the dictionary definition of material wealth. I have come to believe that wealth should be everything that you consider of value. You need money because that's how we exchange things, but money doesn't get you everything. There's a reason the old saying that money doesn't buy happiness has stuck around. You can't put a price tag on it, but the love and support of my wife (Wanda) was critical to the success of our training business, which I could not run it alone. The people who worked with us were also critical to our success, but they don't have a monetary value, either. We've had employees who've been with us for decades and, because we've had good people to help run the business, it has taken stress off of Wanda and me. Over the years, we've built a network of people we could trust, and that reduced our stress and helped us keep us mentally and physically strong. Remember, stress is a killer. That makes those trusted employees more valuable than a sack full of gold. As a horse trainer, I know that if you don't have good horses and good people working with you, then all the money in the world becomes meaningless. Without those trusted people around you, the fanciest barn turns into the empties, loneliest, and most worthless place around. People matter—in life, they are a source of true wealth.

In both the rodeo and horse racing worlds, I saw a lot of people with a lot of money who were a whole lot of miserable. It's clear they were looking for something, but they were looking in the wrong place. Money might be part of the ingredients to wealth but it is only *part* of it. I've seen people with just a few well-managed horses just as happy as the owner of a large stable. At the end of the day, the person with just a few horses knows he has good horses, is doing right by those horses and is well-liked and respected for it. That's real wealth, too.

In addition to learning that wealth is not just money, my other important piece of advice is don't be fooled into believing that wealth automatically brings you happiness. It can help, but only you can know what is in your heart and soul. Money can bring you a sense of material peace, like when it provides food and shelter for you and your family, but it cannot give you spiritual peace. Finding the essence of who you are and following the path God has for you can give you that. Instead, look at wealth as God's gift to you. Your role with that gift is to serve as the earthly steward who uses it for examples of God's blessing. Remember the parable of the faithful servant and his talents? Use it to honor your Master— God—and don't let your ego create a false god of money. Then your wealth becomes a blessing to all.

Chapter 7

CHARITY

Now this I say, he who sows sparingly will also reap sparingly, and he who sows bountifully will also reap bountifully. Each one must do just as he has purposed in his heart, not grudgingly or under compulsion, for God loves a cheerful giver. (2 Corinthians 9:6-7)

When I was younger, I had trouble accepting the responsibilities of wealth. One reason for this was because I did not really understand the concept of charity. Christianity often discusses charity, but what is charity, really? One type of charity is about sharing resources. There are obviously those who have in this world, and those who have not. So what about the man who steals bread to feed his family? Is his sin greater than the man who had bread to spare and did not share? Then the other man with no food for his family would not have had to steal. One can only know the truth of this situation by knowing what is in the heart of each man. The man with all the bread should strive to create opportunities for the poor man to earn what he needs to feed his family. If the poor man decides that he'd rather steal bread than take the opportunity to earn bread, then it tells you that deceit, rather than care for his family, is what really is in his heart. If the man with all the bread does not work to create opportunities for his neighbors to earn what is needed to feed their families, then he is being deceitful and not showing love and concern for his neighbors. If God has entrusted you with His wealth, then He certainly intends you to use it for the betterment of His kingdom. After all, you are only the steward of His resources. In this same way, you must often ask yourself what your motives are, and if what you are doing is in keeping with God's Commandments. The point here is about responsibility of self. The man needing bread has a responsibility to use the opportunities given, but the man with wealth has a responsibility to create those opportunities. It's what you do with your abundance of resources that matters.

Charity, however, is not merely giving money to good causes or sharing your resources. Charity is about you sharing your gifts with others, too, to help them develop their own. This is not about boasting about your accomplishments. It is about you teaching others and learning from others so that each of us can recognize our unique gifts and develop them. If charity were just about giving money, then only the wealthy could be charitable. But if you consider that charity can simply be giving your time or sharing your knowledge to help another person recognize what he or she has been given by God to live a successful life, then you realize that one does not need to be wealthy to be charitable.

To return to an analogy with training horses, charity can be helping people discover their inner talents and then helping them to use those talents to achieve success in life, just as a good horse trainer brings out the talent in each horse and helps it be a success in whatever equestrian discipline best suits that horse. But one of the differences between a good trainer and an inadequate trainer is that a good trainer also knows that he, or she, can *learn* from the horse they are training. Every horse teaches you something, and that lesson helps to carry you forward as a trainer. In other words, the lessons you learn from each horse are lessons that help you succeed with future horses. It becomes a building process.

It's the same with people. What you teach others carries them forward in life just as what you learn from others takes you forward in life. If you think you're too good to learn from others, then you'll be missing many important lessons in life.

So if success is not about becoming rich, what then is success? We have to look at success in a completely different light. Success is simple. It is doing what you love. One person might want to raise three children and give them a good education. If this person forms a family, has children, and finds work that makes it possible for him or her to support those children and educate them, then he or she will be happy. For that person, this will be a successful life.

Peace and contentment with life is success. It is what gives you satisfaction with life and gives you the fulfillment that you are seeking in life. The world looks at material success—how many records we've sold, how much money we have, what kind of car we drive. I look at personal success. I think that Viktor Frankl said it well in *Man's Search for Meaning* when he described a successful life as one in which an older person has actualized the potential he had as a young person. When we are young, life is full of possibilities and God gives us what we need to realize our potential. It is up to us to have realized that potential at the end of our lives. As Frankl puts it:

> *"In the past, nothing is irretrievably lost, but rather, on the contrary, everything is irrevocably stored and treasured.*
>
> *From this one may see that there is no reason to pity old people. Instead, young people should envy them. It is true that the old have no opportunities, no possibilities in the future. But they have more than that. Instead of possibilities in the future, they have realities in the past—potentialities they have actualized, the meaning they have fulfilled, the values they have realized—and*

> *nothing and nobody can ever remove these assets from the past." (Frankl, pp. 150-151)*

True success is finding fulfillment in life and achieving your dreams. But it's important to point out here the difference between wants and dreams. Wants fade away but dreams build and grow and enlarge and become real. Dreams are what come from inside of us and they help push us forward. Wants are usually deceptive because they are what TV and other media advertising tell us we want—"If you own this car, you'll be a big man on the block." People who pursue wants build monuments. People who pursue dreams build lives.

The other problem with wants is that they never end. You can never be at peace because you are always pursuing some new want. As we seek our dreams, we build a world that we enjoy and that is fulfilling our own heaven on Earth. If, in building our dreams, we also help others fulfill their dreams, then that is a true fulfillment of life.

People often ask me if I feel that my own life is a success. I say yes. It is a success, not because everything has always gone right for me, but because no matter what I was doing with my life at any particular time, I tried to discover what truths were being brought forward and kept asking myself where I was being taken and why. I learned to accept that it's okay not to have all the answers all the time. As long as you are searching for the answers to your life, then you are on the right path. I think that everyone should be able to live life this way and I believe that everyone can. That's the reason for this book. I think that others can have the success in life that I've had, even if their success doesn't look anything like mine.

Your dreams might not be the same as my dreams, but they both represent what we each need to be personally successful. I have always done what I thought I loved. Some will say that makes me selfish, but allowing yourself to do what you love actually helps you be a very giving person. Let me explain: let's say that your dream is to be a business owner. You allow yourself this personal dream and begin trying to attain your goal. To build a business, you also need a good accountant, one who understands your dream for the business and works with you to achieve it. Yet as the accountant works with you, he fulfills his dream of being a good accountant, maybe even of launching his own accounting firm, and you are the first client. So everybody works together to build. As your wealth increases, your opportunities to help others also increases; as your dream becomes a reality, it helps fuel the dreams of others. If you build something that is only good for you and use others to achieve it (rather than helping them while they are helping you), then you are being selfish and ultimately, rather than a success, you will be a failure. If you work with others and build your dreams together, you are giving to others as much as they are giving to you.

Chapter 8

NETWORKING

The way you interact with people is important in finding your path to success. Just as you can help others build their dreams, you also need others to help build yours. If you treat people with respect and don't burn bridges, then you are always welcomed back to the places you left. By living an honorable life and treating others with respect, you build a base of people on whom you can rely in times of need, just as they know that they can depend on you. This is a message relayed by Christ many times. We are all made in the image of God so treat others as you would treat Christ. I learned this very early in my career as a bull rider and I continued to practice this in my career as a race horse trainer. If you are following racing meets and want to return to the same tracks year after year, you have to act a certain way to be invited back. This is the basics of networking.

Even though I have said that you must discover and follow your individual path to success, I don't want to imply that you must go it alone. Networking basically means developing contacts with people through your interactions with them, and the bottom line is that you cannot build anything without networking. Building relationships with others is very important, but focus on building networks that link you to people who can assist you in achieving your dreams in return for your assistance with their dreams. As we move through life, people—and networks of people—might come and go, but the point is to be sure that when you do connect with others, it is with others who believe in helping every member of the group achieve his or her individual destiny.

If you want to succeed, you need other people to believe in your dream, too. That means being confident in yourself and what you plan to do in your life. I said earlier that the Ten Commandments are the Truths and serve as guideposts for achieving success and I believe that Christ's explanation of the Commandments can help us use them. Christ said that success cannot be built on material things but only on fulfillment of self. He calls on us to love thy neighbor as we love ourselves. Well, you cannot love your neighbor if you cannot love yourself. If we are made in the image of God then if you love God, you must then also love yourself. Clearly, some forms of self-love are destructive. What I am talking about here is having a more positive view of yourself and believing in your own talents. If you have a positive view of yourself, then you will have a positive view of others. That positive view is what leads you towards building networks in which you work with others so that all of you can grow and achieve your dreams together.

So what's the first step in showing others that you're worth their time? It's a tough one at times: take responsibility of self. You can, and are, constantly changing your life in nanoseconds. From the time you get up in the morning until you go to bed, from the time you are born until you die, your life is changing. Life is like a beautiful prism that changes with every turn, which means that you have constant opportunities to put your life on a better path—*but you* must take responsibility for doing this, and you must also take responsibility when you fail.

From responsibility of self comes an awareness of who we are, an awareness of God's guidance in finding success in life, a reliance on the faith to do what we love, and the strength to learn from adversity. In order to acquire responsibility of self, you must take control over your life and not surrender that power to others, whether that be to other people, to ideas, or to institutions. Christ always taught responsibility of self. As He said "the truth shall make you free," "seek and you shall find," "choose me or deny me." (Peter II, 1, v. 9-10). In each of these verses, He empowers *us* to make the choices that will change the rest of our lives. He doesn't tell us to wait for someone else to make the decisions for us! Yet throughout history, others have wanted power—the church, the government, political rulers, etc.—and people have handed their control over to them.

Let me be clear that I am not saying don't go to church. Here you learn and share with others the joy of a life in Christ. I have already said that Christianity is individualistic, but I do believe that the Church has the important role of helping people discover themselves and learn to be aware of God's guidance in life. There are a multitude of different churches in this world, but they all ought to share a common role, which is to teach the lessons of Christ on how we can live our lives through the wisdom of His teachings, through repentance, and through the hope we receive in Christ's death and resurrection. I believe the church teaches the history and knowledge of the Bible and serves as a place where people can come for education, understanding, inspiration, joy, hope, and repentance. For these reasons, the church is a good place to start in the search for yourself.

What cannot be found in the church, or in government, or anywhere *outside* of God, is truth. So, don't surrender your independence. A priest is there to give you guidance and insight, but you must use your own knowledge to determine what direction to go. There is also a difference between *joining* with others to work together toward common goals and being *led* by others toward their own goals that do not include your goals. Too many people today are led either by their peers, by organizations with which they are involved, by religious leaders, or even by their governments. No matter what form control comes in, some will attempt to use it to gain power over others. So from church to politics, just remember to always think for yourself.

People often hand over control of their lives out of want or fear, so an important step to take on the path to success is take control over your life—accept responsibility of self. Remember, those in power seek to delude us by encouraging us to pursue wants, not dreams. We tend to think that we are sophisticated enough that we will not be brainwashed into things, but this isn't so. In today's world, we are bombarded with advertising of all types telling us what we absolutely must have in order to be happy. So remember: take responsibility for achieving your dreams, and make sure they are your dreams and not ones created for you. Don't justify your dreams against someone else's—make sure that you are being true to yourself.

Chapter 9

JUSTIFY TO GOD ALONE

People feel the need to justify everything they do, and one of the favored ways is to see if someone else is already doing it. We say things like, "Well Charlie does that," or "the priest said it's okay," or "I saw someone else do it," or "my friend so and so told me I should do that." It makes us feel better, safer, that we aren't going at something alone. The problem is that if you spend your life waiting for others to tell you that it's okay to do something or waiting to see someone else do it first, then you'll miss out on living your life. Or, worse yet, you'll always make decisions based on what others think you should do rather than on what you want to do.

One of the main problems with always looking for justification for your decisions is that you give control to others. The need to justify causes you to rethink your choices or change direction even when your instincts tell you not to change course. On a small scale you might buy clothes that you know are right for you. Then someone else tells you those clothes are ugly or they don't suit you, so, you stop wearing them. Now exchange "clothes" for "dreams." Are you going to stop pursuing your dream because someone else doesn't think that dream "fits" you well enough? It's a simple example but we do this over and over in our lives. We don't follow the direction that we know is right for us in life and instead we follow the direction that someone else *tells* us is right for us.

I have a great example of how I did this in my own life. In 1990, I was the winning Kentucky Derby trainer with Unbridled, owned by Mrs. Frances Genter. From the Derby, we went to the Preakness Stakes where Unbridled finished second. Our next targeted race was the Belmont Stakes. After the Preakness, I allowed what was being said in the press to affect my decisions for Unbridled. In other words, I let others control my decisions. The Derby, the Preakness, and the Belmont combined make up what is known in racing as the Triple Crown, and very few horses manage to win all three of those prestigious races. All around me I kept reading and hearing people talk about how hard the Triple Crown is on horses—the effort of doing all three races really wore them out. Through our work together, Unbridled and I had worked out a training program that I knew was best for him, but I allowed all this talk to influence my decisions. Rather than keep Unbridled fit and in a normal work program, a program he was used to and that helped him be the best that he could, I backed off on him. It was the same as if the quarterback stopped practicing before the biggest game of the year. The result was that when we got to the Belmont, Unbridled wasn't fit enough to win that race. He finished fourth.

I'm not one to blubber, but will honestly say that I cried when I came back to the shed row after the Belmont and saw the condition of Unbridled. I had let that horse down. Somewhere inside of me I had felt that if I stuck with my training program, I'd have to justify to everyone why I wasn't backing off and giving the horse a break. I didn't train Unbridled the way I should have because I let the press and hearsay influence how I approached training my horse for the next race. In hindsight, I should have stuck to my training program and not worried about justifying my approach to anyone. I knew my horse, but I listened to the press rather than to Unbridled. I know that with some horses, you do need to back off—but that was not the case with Unbridled. Some horses actually thrive on the Triple Crown and get better with each race (which goes back to my earlier point—know the essence of each horse as an individual). So why did I alter my course of training?

Be aware that there is a difference between getting *guidance* and *advice* from others and being *controlled* by others. If you find yourself always trying to justify your decisions and actions to others, then you are ceding control to them. I am not saying that you should never compromise because I do believe that we must respect one another and work together as a community. What I am saying is that you must think carefully about what you compromise. You must not compromise the essence of who you are.

We all tend to admire people who will not compromise their principles regardless of the personal cost, so take a lesson from them and don't compromise your principles or your very essence. Don't look to justify all of your decisions. First of all, if you are trying to find a justification for your decisions, then you are already attempting to avoid taking responsibility for those decisions. Why would you need to prepare the argument "so-and-so did it too" unless you're already trying to shift responsibility to someone else? In other words, you are not accepting responsibility of self. Secondly, remember that it's your life and if you are moving in the direction God set for you, then you don't need to justify your life choices for anyone. Once you get over this need to justify to others, you will feel free to think and act. You only need to justify your decisions to God, and if one of your decisions violates one of the Ten Commandments, then you ask for repentance. Sometimes, we don't know for sure and only discover afterward that our decision led us to stray from Christ's teachings. But I'll say it again, mistakes are how we learn. If you make one, repent, accept His forgiveness, learn from the mistake, and move on. Cede control to Christ alone, and don't let anyone else direct your path.

Chapter 10

KEEP IT UNDER CONTROL

The need to control my own life and maintain my independence has been a driving force in my life and I believe it has contributed to my success. The feeling of independence is part of what I liked so much about being a professional bull rider. As I said before, once in that chute, there was no one but me, the bull, and God. It was complete freedom. That drive to be independent stayed with me when I began training race horses, and I used that drive to further my dream.

The desire to find independence is really what built the foundation of my horse training business, though I'm equally fortunate in that my wife, Wanda, is a skilled horsewoman and believes in our dream, too. We went into training horses because with our combined skills, we would be totally responsible for our business. We would not be reliant on anyone but ourselves for its success. I went to California Polytechnic State University and I learned to shoe horses, Wanda managed the grooming, and together we worked through the training. This need for independence is also what led me down the path to a more holistic approach for horse care. I didn't want to be dependent on a veterinarian, because a vet didn't have the same interest in the horse as I did. I figured that if I could understand the essence of what made a race horse a race horse, and how to support his essence, then I could help that horse achieve maximum performance. What I didn't want was a reliance on artificial means, like illegal medications. Not only was that bad for the horse, but it also meant loss of control. Once you start overusing medications on your horses, you cede control over the horse to the veterinarian. I never wanted to lose control over my world, which was the horse. This isn't to say that you don't listen to advice from others, like veterinarians, but it means that you take the advice and reflect on it. Don't let advice become directives.

Unfortunately, many people have given up control over their lives. We have become a dependent society. People expect *things* to be given to them—material things, a job, even happiness. We have become dependent on others to do things for us, whether the "other" is a person, government, or religious institution. This fact is reflected in our current political environment in which everyone "wants" something from government. The result is gridlock—everyone fighting to use the government to fulfill his or her own wants. Rather than taking responsibility for building their dreams, people focus on getting others to fulfill their desires. People vote their wants and not their needs. Being handed things without working for it, whether it's a college degree, a house, a car or even a job, sounds great. But the truth is that success in life requires hard work. You can't wait around for someone to give you success. You must make the decision and take the action to pursue your dreams.

In our society, advertising does a very good job of confusing wants and dreams. But advertising focuses on making people want things they don't even need. That is, in making people think that things will fulfill their dreams. The success of advertising is evident in the fact that more and more people are driven to pursue their wants rather than their dreams because they have been made to believe that wants and dreams are one and the same. Remember, when trying to tell the difference, the pursuit of dreams builds while the pursuit of wants destroys. Success in life requires that you separate your needs from your wants. Once you do that, you will begin seeing what your destiny really is.

I believe this dependence on other "things" results from our effort to become what we are not. We are not God, but we keep trying to create God, sometimes in our governments and sometimes in our religious institutions. When you remove God and try to replace Him with government or the church, it fails. Governments and churches cannot rule over or provide everything. The more they attempt to have this total power, the harder they fall. I would argue that in the Dark Ages, the church survived in spite of itself. But it's not just at government levels that we see this abuse of power. This danger even exists on a small scale within neighborhoods, workplaces, industries—everywhere. Be sure that the community you are in isn't leading you down the wrong path. There are more than enough examples of community "leaders" who use the "community" to fulfill his or her own wants rather than the good of all. People are promised everything they want, when in reality none of it is what they actually need. On the other hand, if everyone put God first, then the focus would be on using government to meet the needs of all, on helping people build their dreams rather than helping fill the wants of some at the cost to others.

Here is an experiment to try. Use the following blank page and, for just a moment, pretend that you are God. Write down everything that you would do if you were God. These could be big things such as, "If I were God, I would eliminate all the dictators of the world, and I would make all people do X, Y, and Z," or small things such as, "If I were God, I would build a big house on a beach."

Now look at the list and ask yourself—would you be a God of love or a God of wants? Would you be a God who supplied wants or a God who supplied needs?

This is obviously just an experiment to get you thinking about your motivations, because those motivations will affect your path to success. You are not God and can never be, and neither can the local church or the federal government. Whenever a church or government tries to become God itself, it is abusive and destructive. History has proven this over and over and over. If we try and separate God and state, then the state must become God and yet it cannot replace God. As individuals, if we separate ourselves from God then we must become God, which is something we will never be. Every government that has tried to become God has failed, and if you try to become God, then you will fail as well. God is within you. You are part of God, but you are not God. So rely on Him and get moving!

Chapter 11

BE PROACTIVE, NOT PASSIVE

Many people today live passive lives rather than proactive lives, and even Christianity is being used as an excuse to be passive in life. Yet Christ was not a passive person! He was a doer. We sit back and let things happen to us and simply say, "Ah, it is God's will." But God has given us free will, and every second of our lives we are making decisions that impact the world we are building for ourselves. If you do nothing, that's also a decision, and it will impact the world *you* create and the world in which *you* will have to live. If you choose to do nothing in life, you'll still build a world, but probably not one you want. So why not use your free will to build a life you'll love to live?

God gave you the freedom to choose whether you will take course A or course B in life. Free will then also means that you must accept responsibility for your actions and your life. The plus side of this is that it also means that if you don't like your life, then you can change it. If you are dissatisfied with what you have in life, then *you* change it. That's the essence of the whole deal. If you don't like where you are in life, *you can change it with the help of God.*

Some people will argue that they can't change their lives because they have too many responsibilities—to children, to parents, or to other things. If you have responsibilities, then you take care of them. You have to realize, however, that taking care of these responsibilities actually does bring you satisfaction. It can be part of what makes you feel good about who you are, especially if you are doing this out of love. You might be tired and worn out from taking care of your children or aging parents or an ill spouse, but I bet if you search inside yourself, you will discover that you feel good about doing it. Eventually, the work of raising children or caring for a parent will pass, and you will feel good for having done it. The point here is to understand that sometimes the accomplishment of something—having cared for another—is important and it helps make you the person you are meant to be. That love you show for others is also what helps you build a network of good people.

Free will also means that it is our choice whether we act selfishly or act in ways that build a success for all. Suppose there is an old lady in a house that is in the way of a development project. With one stroke of a pen, you can push her out of her house and pay her a mere $100,000 while you then turn around and sell her property for $1 million. You make a $900,000 profit and the old lady only gets $100,000. But what if she becomes sick and her hospital bills are $300,000 or $400,000? Your other choice is to sell her house for her and give her $900,000 of the money. She has enough to take care of her for the rest of her life and you made $100,000. Both of you gain and you can feel good about creating a partnership that benefits both of you. You have the free will to decide which of these two choices you'll make—take a little and take care of her, or be greedy and leave her in need. The choices you make will have lasting consequences, not just on physical things but also on your spiritual condition. So remember that it's really important that you build your world for the right reasons—because it is a place *you* want to live in and not because you think it will give you something.

When I got to the National Finals Rodeo and ended up third-ranked bull rider in the world, I thought I was super special and invincible. I expected my rodeo accomplishments to give me special recognition and adoration from all. Well, I went home soon after that and I ran into the parents of a former schoolmate. They told me that they had heard I was doing well in the rodeo and I said, "Yea, I'm ranked third best in the world." I expected them to be thrilled for me. Instead, they simply said, "Well, that's great." And then they proceeded to tell me about the new car their son had bought. The number one lesson here is that no one is in your world but you. I realized that rodeo was my world but not everyone else's. I remembered this lesson when I moved on to my horse training career. When you win the Kentucky Derby, it's easy to think that you are on everyone's radar, but it's not true. Yes, people might imitate you and give you special attention for a while, but it soon fades and you're right back where you were before. So remember, your life is your life. It's not everyone else's. So build the life that you want to live! You actually do have the power to do this.

If we take a moment to get past our passive mindset, it becomes obvious that we really do control much of what happens in our lives—we can control whether or not we drink or take drugs or get educated or even how we behave. No, we can't control everything that happens *to* us, but we can control the response *from* us, and that response is usually what dictates how our life turns out. To accept responsibility of self is to become proactive in building your life. Responsibility of self is building your dreams and taking action now and in the future. Personally, I think that many people fear responsibility of self because then they can't blame others for what goes wrong in life.

I know all about being afraid to take responsibility for self. In my bull riding days, I was quick to blame everything outside of me when things went wrong. But when things went right, I took the credit. It was when I reached the top of my success as a bull rider that I realized how wrong I was. I thought getting to the top of my world would bring me fulfillment in life, but what it actually showed me was how empty my life really was. It was a time in my life when I had rejected Christianity and believed that everyone and everything, including the church, was full of deceit and wasn't real. I had no trust of anyone or anything. I thought nothing mattered but having fun every day. I truly believed that if I got to the top of the rodeo world that I would have it all. Well, I got pretty close to the top—third-ranked, to be exact. But the funny thing is that when I got there, I realized how empty it was. How empty I was. I felt like I had given everything to rodeo and that it owed me something back, like continuous adoration and praise for how great I was as a bull rider. Guess what? It didn't. One thing I learned was that if you do something just because you want people to adore you for it, then you are doing it for the wrong reason. When I achieved real success in my rodeo career, I discovered that there was nothing at the top but the hatred and mistrust that I had brought with me. I was so overwhelmed with feelings of disappointment that I felt like I was in hell. I was consumed by a sense of despair as I realized that getting to the top of the rodeo world didn't end the emptiness I had felt in life.

One night in a small town along the rodeo circuit, I went out walking in the middle of the night. I found a church along the way, but it was locked. I kept walking. I found another church, but it was also locked. And then I came to a third church. It was a Catholic church and it was open, so I went in and just sat there. I felt like my world was collapsing. I had reached the top of my rodeo world and found only emptiness so what then, I asked, was there? I no longer knew what I wanted in life, but I knew I didn't like who I was. Sitting in that church, I found my way back to the Christian roots my parents had given me. I prayed to God. "I don't know where I'm supposed to go from here. Can you just take my life and let it be Your life?" Let me tell you, when I prayed those words, I felt like Christ had His arm around me, like a cloak wrapped tight. I was covered by His grace. That night in that church, I did three important things—I took responsibility for my life and the mistakes I had made; I asked God for forgiveness; and I accepted that forgiveness and moved on with my life with a new commitment to let Christ be my guide. My life made a complete change. I won't say this was a moment when everything suddenly turned right, because that's not how it works. But it was a moment when I broke from the past and started toward my future. Once I accepted responsibility for my life, I was able to look back at my mistakes and take lessons from them that I could use in my future. Accepting responsibility for myself, my choices, my motivations...it gave me the freedom to exercise free will and take control of my life. One of the first decisions I made was to go back, get Wanda, and get married (which proved to be one of the wisest decisions of my life). The point here is that if you want to control your own life and be independent, then you must accept responsibility for who you are, where you are, and the decisions that have led you there. But it's not enough to do this one time. Developing responsibility of self is a constant, lifelong walk that you must take if your life is to be successful.

You start the process of developing responsibility of self by asking yourself what you need most in life. The word here is "need," not "want." We can want many things, but what do we really need to be successful and happy? Is it to provide a good education for your children? Is it to develop a talent?

Is it to build an organization that changes the world? We all need different things to feel fulfilled. In Matthew 7:24-27, Christ said to build your house on a solid rock so that when the storms come, it will stand. If you build a false world, one based on your wants and not your needs, then it will crumble. Your world will be a solid rock if it is built on Him, being fully honest to yourself about the gifts He has given you and what you need to do with them to glorify Him. Remember that you also need to create a solid network with others. If you don't have a network to hold you up when the storms come—and they will come—then you will crumble.

Responsibility of self makes us take responsibility for our lives and our actions, how they affect us and also how they affect others. When faced with many choices, how can we know which is the right choice? Put God first in your life. By putting God first, we learn to consider others and in this, we are guided in making the decisions that not only benefit us and the successful world God intends for us to create, but also others on their path to do the same.

Chapter 12

YOU ARE PREDESTINED TO MAKE MISTAKES— AND THAT'S OK!

God said, "I knew you before you were" (Jeremiah 1:5), meaning that God created us all for a specific journey. Your journey is one that only you will take. Others may be involved, but they will not be on the same journey. The paths of others might sometimes cross your path or run parallel to your path, but no one else will ever walk the same path in life as you. What God is saying in the words above is that He has a plan for your life, but it is your responsibility to find the path meant for you and to follow it. That path is your predestination. It is the successful road God has always intended for you. But free will means that the choices you make in life—choices that either put you on that path or off of it—are yours to make. God will not force you down a path, but He will help you if you ask.

I believe that people are born with a sort of predestination. Predestination and destiny can be tricky concepts because some people interpret them to mean that their life is already set in stone from birth, so why bother searching for life and exercising free will? You need to think of predestination as your essence. We are each born with our own individual essence. If we can figure out how to live our lives in accordance with our essence, that is if we live the life predestined for us, then we are in harmony with our inner self. Achieving that feeling of internal harmony and peace is really what succeeding in life is all about. Discovering your personal predestination and living it means that you have successfully filled the role God meant for you, and you will notice that you also are actually doing what you love in life.

Think of it like this: you can take two horses that are physically alike and give them the same training and management program. Yet, the first might be a success in racing and the second a failure. Why? Didn't they have the same training? Weren't they given the same opportunities? What makes the difference is what's *inside* the horse. One has the character and spirit to win and one does not. In other words, one is destined to race and one is not. Still, even destined to win, the horse won't go anywhere unless he steps foot on the track. People are the same way. God has given you special gifts that predestine you for His intended path to success. But if you never start the journey, those gifts won't ever do you any good. If you try to do something that you aren't gifted for, you, like the second horse, will feel nothing but discouragement when you fail.

There are many depressed people in this world and while there are clearly medical reasons for some of that depression, I think the vast majority of people are depressed because they have not discovered their destiny, or the essence of who they are meant to be. Sometimes depression is linked to the feelings of frustration we have when we sense that the life we are living is not really the life we love. We feel trapped. Other times, depression hits at a moment when we become aware that we have mistakenly pursued our wants in life instead of our needs and dreams. Christ said, "You shall know the truth and the truth shall make you free," "seek and you shall find." (John 8:32; Matthew 7:7-8). The truth you must discover is the truth of who you are.

As you search for this truth, pay attention to what is happening around you. Very often, something another person says to you or something that happens around you suddenly makes you realize something about yourself. For me, it was horses that taught me much about myself because horses don't lie. Not only do they tell you rather clearly what they like and don't like, but they are also quick to react to what they sense in you whether that is happiness, anger, insecurity, or confidence. Horses helped me see inside of myself. If you pay attention to how people—and animals—are reacting around you, it will give you a window into your inner self. I remember being very nervous before the Kentucky Derby when I was training Unbridled. One day I walked into the barn and Unbridled looked at me as if to say, "What are you worried about? We're ready." In that moment, I gained my confidence and realized that I really did have the talent and skills needed to train a Derby horse. So, what guides you to the truth about yourself might come from anywhere, so stay alert. Your journey on this earth is to find the truth that is within you. When you do that and then match your life to your true self, you will find success. Through God—the infinite intelligence—we are all connected and as each of us finds our essence and lives according to it, we contribute to the overall glorification of God and the harmony of all.

But you must rely on God to find this harmony. Realize that he has an individual path for you and wants to deal with you on an individual basis. I believe that you can find your path in life—your predestination—if you learn to listen to God and follow His guidance. The best example of this in my life was when I was traveling alone between rodeos one time, and I decided to pull over at a bar and have couple of beers. Some locals in the bar spotted me as loner and started harassing me. We went to verbal exchanges. I decided to ease out the door, but I was expecting these two guys to follow. When I got to my car, I loaded a double barrel and patiently waited.

At that time in my life, I believed that you should always take a stand because that was the only way to win. My attitude was that I was justified in not letting anyone push me around. But that time, a voice deep inside me began pushing me to leave in urgency. I listened to that inner voice, put my gun away, and drove off. God speaks to us in those quiet, individual voices inside us all. It is those feelings within you that are what you must learn to become aware of and heed if you are to find your life path and stay on it.

I have looked back at that incident at that bar many times and thought of how my life could have changed if I had made a different decision. My predestination would not have changed, only the path would have changed—and not for the better. I suspect that had I made the other choice and found myself in prison for perhaps the rest of my life, I would still have spent my time in reading and reflecting. Perhaps I would also have written a book like this, but the experiences and perspectives on which I would have drawn for the book would have been greatly different. Who knows? Maybe it would have been about how to avoid *missing* your path to success instead of how to *find* it. But remember, just because we get off track doesn't mean that God can't help us fulfill our greater purpose.

On our journey in life to fulfill our predestination, we will have failures and successes, but both bring us closer to God our Father. They also remind us of how we need His love, forgiveness, and wisdom to guide us. As our lives interact with other people, our past successes and failures can also help guide them in their lives, because it is true that we can learn from the failures and success of others. That is one of my hopes with this book—that you will learn from my failures and successes as you search for the life you were meant to lead. One of the keys to success in building your own world for success is to embrace the adversities that come to you in life because adversity helps guide us to where we are meant to go.

Never forget that failures are a part of life, that setbacks help us realize our finite limits, and that we cannot overcome those limits without God's infinite intelligence. As Christ said "Seek and you shall find, knock and it shall open" (Matthew 7:7). We're human and we are going to mess up, but that's why Christ came to die for us! When you fail, seek God's guidance more, and ask for His help to learn from that failure. But don't be afraid of it.

So many people are afraid of failure that they don't even try. I was sixteen when I got on my first bull. It was at our ranch, and I think I rode him for only two or three bucks. That was a failure, but it didn't keep me from getting back on. In bull riding and in life, every time you get dumped, you are given an opportunity to learn what not to do the next time. If you quit every time life throws you off, then you'll never find success.

Once you are willing to accept failure, you will find the confidence to try new things and take first steps. Remember that we cannot always reason our way to things. You have to rely on faith and the invisible, which means sometimes taking that first step in life where you just go for it. There is no ending to where you will or can go. I've made a lot of mistakes in my life, but looking back, I realize that if I hadn't made some of those mistakes, I wouldn't be where I am. If you never put your hand on a hot stove, you might never face the pain of being hurt. But you also never learn the benefits that the appliance can bring, or the valuable lessons that the mistake could teach you.

I really believe in the theory that *you cannot fail in life, you can only learn,* because out of mistakes comes understanding. Each failure along your path to success is just an opportunity to learn, which takes you closer to success. Those missteps can help you either figure out how to succeed at what you initially set out to accomplish or they can teach you that what you are trying to accomplish in life isn't really the path for you. Either way, failures help to guide you if you reflect on them and learn from them.

One of the important things these learning failures do is they help you discover your unique attributes and talents. These are the gifts God gave especially to you to help you succeed in life. As I said before, one of the central needs in my own life has been independence. Early in life, I decided that having my own business was the best path to finding this freedom. But the question for me was, what type of business? This is where discovering the unique talents and skills God gives to each of us is important for putting you on your path to success. I discovered early in life that I had a way with animals—that is, I had attributes and talents that made me successful in work involving animals. So the best path for me to develop a business and obtain independence was a business that involved working with animals. Wanda and I both had a love for horses and talents in working with them, so training horses was the perfect fit for us. What you must do is discover your special strengths and talents given to you by God, and then use them to create your path to success.

Christ is knocking on your door, ready to come in and help you use your talents. He calls to us, "Here I am! I stand at the door and knock" (Revelation 3:20). Now all you need to do is open the door.

Chapter 13

THE TRUTH SHALL SET YOU FREE

Successfully discovering your own essence—the truth of who you are—requires honesty. Christianity teaches that we should not sin, but what really is sin? My personal belief is that the essence of sin is deceit. What do I mean by this? Well, here is an example. You act as if you are following God's Commandments and therefore, appear to be an exemplary Christian. However, you are not following God's guidance to please God but rather in order to convince others that you are a wonderful Christian so that you can gain their trust or support. Being outwardly Christian becomes a way to gain favor and power rather than honor God. This is my view of the essence of sin—deceit is in the heart and while that might be hidden to other people, it is not hidden from you or God.

It is not only God and others whom we try to deceive. We also try to deceive ourselves. Self-deceit is one of the greater obstacles to success because until we are honest with ourselves about who we are and what we need for fulfillment, we will never be a success. There are many sins that one can commit, but I think one of the worst is being a habitual liar, because it involves living a life of deceit and sin. If you are on drugs, you can quit. If you are lazy, you can get yourself moving and get motivated. But if you are a habitual liar, the danger is that you keep making up so many stories that you get sucked into the world of deceit that you have created. You most certainly have built your own world, but it's not one that will bring you peace of mind. If you want to build a successful life, then avoid deceit toward others and toward yourself. You must first know yourself and you must know your dreams and these must be your real dreams, not wants masquerading as dreams.

Pursue the truth of what you really love to do and you will find happiness. Beware of pursuing what is false—wants—rather than what is true. Here is an example of falseness. You get a $50,000 winner in racing and, all of sudden, you get excited about the money and you want a $100,000 winner. This now becomes your thought pattern. You win one thing and start wanting the next bigger thing. After I trained Unbridled and won the Kentucky Derby, I went from loafers to wingtip shoes—for me that meant I was able to chase bigger things! But when people asked me if I was going to build a bigger stable of horses and move on up in the world of racing, I reflected and thought, "Even though I'm now wearing wingtip shoes, I think I'll stay with the people who liked me when I wore loafers."

I felt that if I had gotten bigger, I would have lost myself, period. I would not have been who I am. Maybe I might have had more wins, but who I was would have disappeared. I'm not saying people who grow their stable and have a lot of horses in their stable are wrong, but it was not who *I* really was. It wasn't right for *me*. We can't really say that one person is wrong to build a big stable or that another one is right because he remained small. What is right for one is not always right for another. My philosophy is that you build your own world and it is not the same as someone else's world. Christ teaches us how to build every world correctly and if we ask, He will show us how to build the world that is right for us.

This process of building our own world and discovering the essence of who we are is a life-long endeavor. Even at this point of my life, I have sometimes had to find my way back to the truth of who I am. I've had to ask myself, what is the satisfaction of training race horses, why do this with my life? Is it about getting trophies and being on top of the game and winning? For some trainers, this is what drives them, and I admit there have been times in my life when I thought these were the goals of being a trainer—but I was deceiving myself. While these might be the things that are right for some trainers, they were not the things that really brought me joy and satisfaction in working with horses. In time, I discovered that what I truly enjoyed was the challenge of beating the odds. My real passion was the search for understanding the horse. In time, I realized that the horse is very simple. He will tell you what he likes and dislikes. What I most enjoy is the process of learning how to listen and hear the horse and learning the art of being patient and letting the horse teach me.

The philosophy and approach of some other trainers doesn't fit me, so I have created my own philosophy and am happily experimenting with my own approach to training. I have spent much time exploring acupuncture diagnostics and chiropractic techniques as well as energy balancing to optimize the well-being of horses. It's an approach that fits my interest in connecting the mental, physical, and spiritual in horses and humans. The point is that I am pursuing the truth of who I am and not trying to be like other trainers, which, in my case, would be deceptive because it would not be the truth of who I am as a trainer.

This brings me back to my point that the search for self requires that we be quiet in our minds and our soul so that we can feel the Holy Spirit and be guided. The Holy Spirit "proceedeth from the Father and the Son"—that is the number one point. John 16:13-15 states, "Now be it that He, the Spirit of the truth, is come, He will guide you into all truth for He shall not speak of Himself but whatsoever He shall hear, that shall He speak and He will show you things to come. He shall glorify Me, for He shall receive of Mine and shall show it unto you. All these things that the Father hath are Mine; therefore said I that He shall take of Mine and shall show it unto you"

The verses are Christ's promise to us that God shows Him all things and He then tells them to the Holy Spirit and it is from the Holy Spirit working within us that we also come to know all things. This includes coming to know our own individual essence. If we quiet ourselves so that we can feel and hear the Holy Spirit, then we have a direct link to the infinite intelligence of God. Christ tells us that God will give us whatever we need to find success in our lives, but these things will come to us when we are ready for them:

> "Verily, verily I say unto you, he that believeth on Me, the works that I do shall he do also, and greater works than these shall he do because I go unto my Father. And whatsoever ye shall ask in My name, that will I do that the Father may be glorified in the Son. If ye shall ask anything in My name, I will do it" (John 14:12-14).

This saying above links back to the importance of understanding. You must first have understanding before God will give you what you need for YOUR success. And the key word above is "glorified." The life you are meant to live is one that will be in harmony with God because it will be a life that contributes to the overall glorification of God. If you ask things in God's name that are not for the right reasons—for the glorification of God—then you will not receive them. Ask for the right reasons and you will receive what you need. If you do things for reasons that in your heart are pure, God will know it, even if society judges you for your choices.

We must be careful of how we judge others. As it says in the Bible, "Judge not that ye be not judged. For with what judgment ye judge, ye shall be judged; and with what measure ye mete, it shall be measured to you again" (Matthew 7:1-2). Certainly it is very clear that a society must exact justice against those whose deceit harms others. But we must also allow for forgiveness and acceptance of mistakes. We all make mistakes and this is where repentance comes into play. Without it, we keep living a deceit and we will never be able to put our lives back on the track to whatever our success is meant to be. Fortunately, we have Christ who, through His death and resurrection, brought us the repentance that makes forgiveness and a new life possible. As I have said already, put God first. If you put God first, then you will automatically ask for things in truth and not in deceit. If you ask in truth and sincerity, then you will never be without God's help in the form of strength and wisdom from Him, and He will guide you down your path to success.

Chapter 14

INTUITION

This journey of life is not easy, but not only will God give you what you need to find your own success, but He also will lighten the load when you need help, if you ask. As Christ told us, "Come unto me, all ye that labor and are heavy laden and I will give you rest. Take my yoke upon you and learn from me; for I am meek and lowly in heart and ye shall find rest unto your souls. For my yoke is easy and my burden is *light*" (Matthew 11:28-30).

I will say it again—you can find success in life because God has given you all that you need to find it, but it is up to you to look for your life and seek God's help. That help might come in pieces. Remember, Christ has told us that we will be given what we need when we are ready for it and can understand it. If you ask for something but can't yet grasp it, God won't give it to you until you understand it and seek it for the right reason. When you are ready, you will receive what you need from God. He knows what you need. He is just waiting for the moment when YOU understand what you need and then ask for it. This moment of awareness on your part can come suddenly. Sometimes you just feel it in your mind and all of a sudden you know where you need to go or what you need to do. Other times it comes as events and things just appear in your life. When you look back you can recognize these signs, but at the time they happened, you didn't. Things will evolve around you that can all of a sudden make you understand what you need or don't need (but once thought you did).

In some ways, feeling what is right is about intuition. We talk about intuition and instinct a lot and it is important to understand the differences between the two. They can guide you in the right direction or the wrong direction. Instincts are like unconscious, rapid reactions to external stimuli. When a horse feels threatened, it runs. Taking flight is the natural instinct of a horse when it feels danger. Understanding the natural instincts of a horse is the first step on the path to training it. Like horses, people have instinctive reactions as well, and they can even be developed. For example, riding bulls is dangerous and nearly every bull rider has the injuries to prove it. Every time you ride a bull, you put yourself in a life threatening situation. However, a rider learns with each bull ride and, over time, the body instinctively reacts to lessen the chances of injury. In other words, your body learns new responses based on past responses that caused injury. This is rather common in most physical pursuits. The more you do something, the more your body develops instincts that automatically take over. Instinct is a sort of learned reaction to responses. These can be physical—such as in sports—or mental. If you consistently put God first in your life and respond to things around you with honesty and truth, then in time that is how you will instinctively respond to everything.

Intuition is somewhat similar in that it is a feeling one gets that is not necessarily conscious thought. It's like an immediate insight you have about a situation, sort of like an unconscious knowledge. The difference between instinct and intuition is that we have time to reflect on our intuitions and consider how best to use them. The thing with intuition is that you must ask yourself if this unconscious feeling that is trying to guide you is driven by a hidden want that you have or coming from a need. Is it good or is it bad? If you are faced with two choices and something inside tells you take choice A, is it desire making you want to choose A or is it actually the correct course of action? Use intuition to help guide your choices in life, but always ask if the intuition is building dreams and providing benefit or simply fulfilling some want within you. Measure intuition against the Ten Commandments. Does the intuition guiding you violate any of those Commandments? If your intuition is unconscious knowledge coming from the Holy Spirit to guide you, then it will send you in the right direction. To know if that intuition is the voice of the Holy Spirit, read the words of Christ in Matthew, Mark, Luke, and John. Put God first. And most of all, learn to quiet the world around you. In our modern world, it seems that we are inundated constantly with noise. Learn to be silent. Be quiet. Listen to the inner voice. Get a cup of coffee and just sit with yourself. Far too often people seek constant action and activity because they don't want to think. They don't want to hear the inner voice. They want to shut it out. Be patient. Intuition is often like wine. If the intuition is good, it'll get clearer and better with time. If it's bad, it'll turn to vinegar.

The mind is an amazing thing. Thinking is very powerful, but people don't spend enough time thinking. Everyone is too busy doing. Imagine what it would be like if you spent one week doing nothing but thinking; if you could put aside all your business and personal affairs so there was nothing to focus on but pure thought. It would be amazing what your mind could do if freed from all the clutter.

So, take time to contemplate. Don't let your senses be too bombarded. In my own journey as a youth, I found it best to take Heaven and Hell out of the whole equation, because the worry about where I was headed distracted me. I felt that I didn't want to sit around my whole life and say, 'I did this really well or do that then I'll be in Heaven.' From the start, I didn't like the explanation of Heaven. When I was a teenager, I wanted to ride bulls. I didn't care about playing the harp and singing. So I ignored them and studied what Christ said in the Bible. Once you take out Heaven and Hell, you realize that truth is in Christ's teaching and that peace and understanding are all that you are really after.

I am not trying to start a scholarly debate about Heaven and Hell and scripture. The truth is all that I am after because I believe that if you have truth, then you have peace and understanding.

Chapter 15

LET EVENTS TAKE YOU WHERE YOU ARE MEANT TO GO

Through contemplation we discover the guidance of the Holy Spirit within us. Through events that impact us both externally and internally, the Holy Spirit guides us. Events in your life will take you where you are going if you learn to embrace them and reflect on them so that you can understand their lessons. All events are absolutely necessary and helpful, even ones of adversity. Some events feel good because they are like victories, but I will tell you this—you will learn more from those events that are adversity. The victories are just sort of a pat on the back. The adversity comes so you can learn from your mistakes and be redirected. It is through this learning that you gain true knowledge.

We live in a world of people searching for understanding, searching to make sense of the events that happen in their lives, and searching for love. Have you ever seen that bumper sticker, "My Dog Loves Me"? Maybe it's even on your car. Well dogs are great animals. They soothe us when we're upset and make great listeners when we have problems to talk about. We're all looking for someone to speak with and to love and to give us answers, but in all honesty, it's not the dog. It's God. He is there and He is talking to us and He is trying to guide us through His words and through the events of life. Your job is to watch for those events in your life that are meant to guide you, and learn from them. When I was inducted into the National Museum of Racing and Hall of Fame, some people asked me what I was going to do now that I had reached that milestone. I said that I was going to do what I've done all my life—*I'm going to where I'm being taken.* All my life I have tried to learn from the events that were meant to lead me to where I need to go.

I once had the most unusual day while I was driving to Chicago, and my mind was just wandering as it often does on long drives. But that day, I had a moment of clarity. A God-moment, if you will. Like a rapid slide show, pictures of my past started appearing in my mind, and suddenly I could understand why those moments mattered. It was instantaneous moments of complete understanding. Just like that, I could see everything that had happened during my life and understood why it happened. That experience made me very aware that every event in my life was leading me somewhere, even if I didn't understand it at the moment it happened.

My advice here is, pursue what you love and events will guide you to where you are going. I took this approach to life the moment I woke up on my first day after high school graduation. Lying there in bed, I asked myself, "Okay, big shot. You're out of high school, so now what?" I lay there thinking for about five minutes and I decided to do what I felt I would love doing, and at that time, I wanted to rodeo, to ride bulls. I was successful as a bull rider, in some ways. I wasn't as good as I could have been, but I learned a lot from being a bull rider, and the things that happened to me from pursuing that took me to where I am now. For one, I met life-long friends from following the rodeo circuit. If it were not for what the rodeo circuit taught me, I might never have been a success as a horse trainer. Life on the rodeo circuit taught me the importance of building a network of true friends. You never knew when you might need to borrow twenty bucks to get to the next town. And if I hadn't met Wanda while following the rodeo circuit, I would not have had the benefit of her love and valuable horsemanship skills. Do what you love and along the way, you will gain what you need in order to be a success. If my life proves anything, it's that events will keep pushing you along to where you need to go.

Some of you may be reading this and thinking, "Well, he just got lucky. Maybe it worked for him, but it certainly wouldn't work for me!" So here's where I must say that I don't believe in coincidence. Events happen and people come into your life for a reason. If you reflect back on events or people that have passed through your life, you will come to understand their role. Every move you make in life will have an impact, and that's why you need to take time to think and assess your life.

Chapter 16

THE VALUE OF ADVERSITY— LEARNING FROM YOUR MISTAKES

The best remedy for those who are afraid, alone, or unhappy is to go outside somewhere they can be quiet, alone with the Heavens, nature, God. Because only then does one feel that all is as it should be.—Anne Frank (1929-1945)

You cannot be on an eternal high all the time. I learned this when I was riding bulls. One day, you're one of the best bull riders in the world and feel like you're on top of the world. The next day, you hit bottom. You must learn to accept adversity in life and embrace adversity for what it can teach you. I realized that on the night when I went walking in that small town I mentioned before, where I sat in that church and found my way back to Christ. People who can't embrace adversity tend to blame everyone and everything around them for what is wrong in their lives. Once you accept adversity, then you stop blaming other things, accept responsibility of self, and begin to learn from your hardships.

It's hard to explain what it's like when you really hit bottom in life until you hit it. Some people never hit bottom because they're smart enough to avoid it, usually because they learned from watching others. But most of us hit a wall at some point. That's actually a good thing, because it makes you stop and reflect on your life. And very often, it's an adversity that makes you change course—often for the better. Even if everything seems to be going your way, you will face adversity because you can't stay at the top forever. I hadn't learned this when I was riding bulls, and getting knocked off the top of my bull riding world nearly destroyed me. When I had my Derby win with Unbridled, I remembered this lesson from my bull riding days and was more careful not to let the success go to my head. And sure enough, the fame from that win soon faded. By the time of my Kentucky Derby win with Street Sense, this lesson had really sunk in and I handled that period of fame much better than any times in the past.

I'm not saying that you shouldn't strive for huge successes in your life. I'm saying don't make those successes the sole goals of your life. Appreciate those successes, because they are often signs that you're on the right track in life, but don't stress yourself out trying to stay at the top 24/7. Success will not protect you from the tribulations of life and you must accept that tribulation is just a part of life. There is no getting around that fact, but tribulations can be overcome. As Christ said, "In the world you shall have tribulation, but be of good cheer. I have overcome the world" (John 16:33). Pick up the morning newspaper or watch the evening news and it is clear to you that the world really is full of trials and hardships. However, you can sometimes choose whether or not these affect you by deciding whether or not to participate in them. At the moment that you participate—mentally, physically, or spiritually—it becomes an event in your life.

If an earthquake hits in a far-off country and you ignore it, then that tribulation is not an event in your life. But, if you go to that country and assist with disaster response or organize a fundraiser to send aid to the region, then you have in some way participated in that tribulation. It now becomes an event in your life that in some way will affect you. Even if all you do is think about that disaster and it causes you to change the way you prepare your family to deal with a similar disaster, then you have participated in that tribulation and it becomes an event that caused change in your life. How much the tribulation becomes an event that affects you often depends on how much you participate in it.

But while you can choose whether or not to participate in some tribulations, there are others that you can't ignore and you must accept them, face them, and learn from them. Sometimes the effect of a tribulation is so immense—the earthquake could be in your own town—that you are forced to participate. Or, the tribulation happens directly to you, like a death in the family, a car accident, or getting injured (which I often experienced riding bulls). Sometimes you can't avoid involvement in some of the tribulations of this world, but how those tribulations affect you is based on how you respond to them and *that is in your control.*

No one wants adversity in life, but we can't avoid it. I have said before that it is during times of adversity that we learn. One problem with adversity is that we misunderstand what it is. Let's consider the definition in the *Merriam-Webster* dictionary—adversity is defined as hard times or misfortune. If we accept the dictionary definition, then we tend to assume that if adversity is sent our way from God, then it must be punishment for transgressions. I believe in a different definition of adversity. I believe that adversity is God's way of redirecting us and reminding us that everything earthly is temporary—wealth, material possessions, health, even life itself. Adversity makes us stop and appreciate what we do have. It makes us recognize what blessings we have and consider the things we need to change.

If you can accept my understanding of adversity, then I believe it will give you a whole new focus. Adversity makes you realize that all earthly things are temporary and that only God is permanent. If you put your hopes on having money in the bank, there is a good chance that somehow it will disappear anyway, and you will be reminded that having money can be temporary. Christ advised us to store our treasure in Heaven, not on Earth, "For where your treasure is, there your heart will be also" (Luke 12:34).

Don't sell out your soul, your dreams, or who you are for a fleeting, earthly treasure. You are too special to give up who you are. Everybody goes through these bad phases in life and you will get through them, but not without faith and hope. You will face many tribulations in life, but faith is what will give you the understanding to turn those adversities into the lessons that will take you closer to the essence of who are you—the destiny God has placed within you.

Some might ask how I can write about adversity when I haven't experienced all the adversities of life. True, I've never been through a tornado, lost my house to a fire, or a child to an accident, but I have had my own share of adversities. We all have some adversities and they are all reminders that everything earthly is temporary—money, material possessions, trials, even life itself is temporary. Yet one thing is for certain: you are not alone in having to overcome times of tribulation. I have great respect for the wisdom of Mother Theresa, who saw so much of the world's pain and said that the only way through them is to have hope, which comes through grace. You will have doubt, but keep in mind the saying that "this too shall pass" holds true. As the pendulum swings left, come to neutral, because it will come back right. The best strategy when things go bad is to gather your resources around you, come to neutral, and wait.

If an adversity is of your own making—and often they are—then repent, ask God for forgiveness and guidance, accept His forgiveness, learn from the adversity, and get your life back on track. I can't emphasize enough the importance of the concept of forgiveness. We are human. We make mistakes. But God's grace grants forgiveness so that we can hit a wall and find our way back, no matter how bad our downfall. Accept responsibility and allow God to lead you on.

The important thing to understand here is that Christ died for our sins and this means that ever since the coming of Christ, God does not punish until the final judgement day. I really believe this and it tells me that adversity is not God sending us a punishment. It is simply His reminder that everything earthly is temporary and adversity helps to bring us back to God's true love and blessing. If we doubt this, if we think that adversity is punishment, then I say that is a clear sign that Satan has intervened with deceit (sin) and caused us to doubt and feel anguish. Do not let anyone tell you that your adversity is punishment. It is not. It is guidance, for you and others that you can help. I'll give you some examples.

For one, think about the mistake I mentioned earlier with Unbridled after our Kentucky Derby win. I changed my training program for the horse because I listened to all the talk about how physically demanding the three Triple Crown races were on horses. Rather than doing what I knew was right for that particular horse, I backed off because everyone said he needed a lighter training schedule. It was a big mistake. By the Preakness Stakes, I had a little less horse than I should have and we placed second. By the Belmont Stakes,

Unbridled was basically unfit and we finished fourth. That poor showing in the Belmont was a real adversity in my life, but I did three important things after that event that turned that adversity into a later success. First, I took responsibility for the loss—I had made the decision to change my training program. Accepting responsibility made it possible for me to recognize that just as I had the power to make wrong choices, I had the power to make right choices. This is where free will comes in, because I also had the free will to make new decisions, and that is exactly what I did. The second important thing I did was recognize that I could choose to stop listening to others. I did, and I went back to listening to my horse and myself. I made the decision to go back to the training program that I believed was right regardless of what others thought. The third thing I did was reflect on my mistakes and the resulting adversity so that I could learn from it. I realized that some horses actually thrive on the pressure of the Triple Crown.

I was so confident of my ability to learn from this adversity that I publicly made a promise to Unbridled's owner, Mrs. Genter, and to the press that we would return and we would win the Breeders' Cup Classic in New York in the fall. I didn't get mad at others or even at myself for my mistake. The best way to approach mistakes is to calm down and refocus—learn from the mistake, prepare for the next step, and go on. My entire focus after the Belmont was on preparing Unbridled for the Breeders' Cup. When race day came, we drew the 14th post position, which was about the worst position one could draw, and the press said we had no chance of winning. But I had learned not to listen to the press. We won the Breeders' Cup and Unbridled became one of only two horses in history, at that time, to win both the Kentucky Derby and the Breeders' Cup Classic in the same year. My experience with Unbridled taught me to listen to my horse, not to the press or the public. When Street Sense came along, the press and public said that a horse couldn't win the Derby coming in with only two prep races, but Street Sense disagreed. He was telling me that he could do it. I listened to him, we went for the Derby, and he won. The horse knew and, because I had learned from my mistake with Unbridled, I listened to him.

Another example of the value of adversity comes from my bull riding days. I once drew a bull that was an average ride. The ride went well, but when I went to step off the bull, he threw my left leg into a light pole and fractured it. The result was that I was temporarily out of work and wondering what could go wrong next. A contractor offered me a judging position in Coffeyville, Kansas, which I was glad to do since it meant some income to supplement my living. On my first night, I was judging bareback bronc riding and the first horse out came charging straight at me. I was still on crutches, so I wasn't very mobile. It became clear the horse was about to run me down. At the last moment I was able to move away from the horse, having to abandon crutches and swinging my left leg clear. All seemed well except that instead of the horse kicking straight out behind, it cow kicked and nailed my left leg. The result was a compound fracture, and a rod had to be inserted from my knee down to my ankle.

Now at this point, I was really beginning to ask what more could go wrong in my life, and I was certain that if you believed in luck, Lady Luck was definitely not on my side. About three months later, I received a letter from Uncle Sam: you have been reclassified 1A, please report to Amarillo, Texas and bring an overnight bag. At the time, there was this little thing going on a place called Vietnam. I had a lot of friends who had been drafted and sent off already, and while I was not aware of everything they went through in that battle, I knew it was not good.

I called the doctor who had performed my surgery so that my x-rays and medical records could be sent to my local draft board. Once they saw all the damage, I was reclassified as 4F—not fit for duty. The accidents and resulting physical damage that I thought were ruining my life might have actually saved it. My injuries kept me from being drafted and sent to Vietnam. As I said, everything happens for a reason.

You can look at these events in my life—the bull throwing me into a light pole, the horse kicking my leg—and call it tribulations at the time or luck in hindsight. I'm not sure what you want to call it—personally I don't believe in luck—but I do know that events happen in order to take us places. We should pay attention to the events in our lives because there is a message in them even if we don't see it right away. At the time of these accidents, I could not see how they could possibly be a positive thing in my life or understand how they would impact my life in a good way, but I came to understand it afterward. Much of life is like that. You must reflect on events in your life because there is a message in there somewhere. Events help show us who we are and where we are meant to go. We are on a journey and it is the most exciting journey we can possibly take—a journey to discover our unique essence. It is through that journey that we can find the talents and skills God has given us to live a successful life, a life that adds to the glorification of God.

My cousin's son, a wounded warrior, is another example of the value of adversity and how it can serve God's greater purpose. This young man and his family have faced tremendous adversity but, like many other similar families that have faced tragedies, they have turned the adversity into something positive. They have become leaders in helping others to learn from their similar adversity and get through it. Families like that of my cousin have used their tragedies to build organizations that now better the lives of others who are facing the same challenges. And, because they have done this, others are not facing their tragedies alone. In other words, the adversity faced by some means that others are now better off.

And remember when Jesus healed the blind man in John 9:1-3? God tells us clearly there that even tribulations can be used to point to God's goodness.

> *And as Jesus passed by, he saw a man which was blind from his birth. And his disciples asked him saying, Master, who did sin, this man, or his parents, that he was born blind?*

> *Jesus answered, Neither hath this man sinned, nor his parents: but that the works of God should be made manifest in him.*

We need to view adversity as a learning lesson and always remember that, through adversity, God moves us forward to our main goal in life—discovering the essence of what we were meant to be and then living the life we are meant to live. Understanding who we really are is what brings us into a deeper relationship with Christ. Remember that in the Triune God (Father, Son, and Holy Ghost) there is love, compassion, forgiveness, and infinite wisdom. These things can help us live lives of creative accomplishments in His glory. As you build your earthly world, through the study of His words and through prayers, you will realize that as Christ said in John 8:32, "You shall know the truth and the truth shall make you free."

I've never learned much when a horse wins a race, but I can tell you that I learn a lot when he loses. It's the loss that makes me reassess what I'm doing, and from that comes a new approach that often leads to winning the next race, as my story of Unbridled showed. You don't learn much from success, but you learn a lot from failure. That's why there really isn't any such thing as failure. There are only lessons. So if you ask me what I believe is the key to success, I will tell you that it is adversity. When I look back at my life, it was when I embraced adversity that I then found success. If you don't learn to embrace the adversities in your life, you will never succeed. It's as simple as that.

Adversity often comes when you chase your wants and God is trying to redirect you. It's about helping you discover that what you actually need in life to be happy isn't the same as what you thought you wanted. We all know the saying, "take a lemon and make lemonade," and it is so true. If you learn from your mistakes, then you can never fail—you can only learn. In training horses, I learned that a top race horse can overcome adversity. The ability to overcome adversity is what separates a champion race horse from the others. It's the same with people. Those who can overcome adversities in life are the ones who succeed.

Christ said choose me or deny me. If you choose Him, then you gain the faith and strength to go on and the understanding to see what adversity is teaching you. You will then discover what it is that God has planned for your life and you will begin to build your world—the one God wants you to build. By choosing Christ, you gain the faith that God's grace will lead you to the essence of what you are meant to be. You can only find this by exercising your free will and making yes or no choices when faced with circumstances that are laid before you as you go through life. When you make the wrong choice but have Christ within you, then other circumstances will arise that will lead you back to where you need to be. In other words, the events that occur in your life will take you where you need to go. On the other hand, if you are out there on your own and follow a path that takes you to a dead end, that's real adversity. When that happens, you must turn around and put yourself back on the path of seeking God first.

The courage to do what you love will come when you accept that you cannot fail, that you can only learn. I've been blessed with success beyond what I imagined. At this point in my career as a horse trainer, I don't need more trophies for the mantel. I've looked back at my life in an effort to understand why and how I was so blessed and I believe that others can be just as blessed. It is my goal now to share with people how they can build their own world and move on to living a successful life. Events take place for a reason, so study the events in your life—the things that happen and the people you meet. Things happen to us for a reason. We meet people for a reason. Reflect on this. I have a philosophy in life which is that everything that seems simple is actually very complicated. A simple event, such as meeting someone, can result in a host of changes in your life.

Having said all of this, I don't want to give the impression that predestination means that you go sit under a tree and things will just happen. Free will means that you have choices and decisions to make. God gave you what you need so that you could go out there and build your life, but doing it is up to you. It is when you believe in God that you gain faith, and when you have faith, you have the courage to go for your life. Will you face adversity if you go out there and pursue your dreams? Yes, of course, but remember that if you don't go for it and sometime hit adversity, then how will you ever learn? How can you ever understand or not understand? Different situations will push you in the direction you are going if you will learn from the events in your life.

In some way, God is in control of everything, and by understanding and accepting that we can find what we need in order to overcome loss. As Christ said, "These things I have spoken unto you, that in me ye might have peace. In the world ye shall have tribulation: but be of good cheer; I have overcome the world" (John 16:33).

I will say it again—we must look at adversity as a learning lesson and always remember that God is moving us forward to our main goal in life, which is to have a deeper relationship with the Triune God. As I've said with regard to my own life, I am going where I am being taken. Once I gave my life to God, events moved me, though I did have free will to choose which way to proceed. Sometimes, not trusting in God, I moved in a direction and it soon became evident that my choice had been bad. Surprisingly, at those times, other events then occurred that moved me back in the correct direction. And very often, the event that put me back on course was one that was an adversity. Adversity made me stop moving and forced me to think, pray, and accept the trials I had to face. It was difficult to accept the adversity when it occurred, but those were the times in which I learned the most and advanced the most. You will come to realize as you go through life that all things really do work for the glory of God—"For He is not a God of the dead, but of the living: for all live unto Him" (Luke 20:38).

Chapter 17

BRINGING IT ALL TOGETHER FOR A LIFE OF SUCCESS

The search for self is an individual journey. I can't say this enough. If you quiet yourself and study scripture, then you will sense the guidance from the Holy Spirit. The final decisions on what to do in life come from inside of you. I tell people it's like hip replacements. A doctor once told me long ago that you can't diagnose when people need one. If you really need it, you'll know. It's that way with much in life. If you really need something, you'll know it. Sometimes you feel like you are ready to make a move in life, but the door to move through doesn't open. That's okay. It tells you that it's not really time to make a move. If and when you are meant to go elsewhere, a door will open. No one can really tell you if, when, or how to make changes in your life. *Face this fact— no one can tell you the essence of who you are but you. God knows and He'll show you when you are ready to listen and ready to act.* When decisions are the right ones, you will know it. The reason I'm so much in favor of Christianity is because it's the only religion that leads you back to self with one statement—if you study Christ's teaching, "you shall know the truth and the truth shall make you free" (John 8:32).

Put God first, do what you love, and learn from your mistakes. That's it. We are all on a journey of learning and the whole key to life is to find the essence of self, which can only be found through God. You need to shut out the noise of life and listen in order to put your life on the path meant for you. Some people think that Christianity makes people meek and weak. I promote Christianity in this book because I believe the opposite. Christianity makes you strong.

I've heard some say that if God is so strong, then why didn't He send Christ to lead armies against evil? This question comes from people who don't understand Christianity. Christianity is not about God doing things for us. God gives each of us, through His grace and love, the free will and the talents we need in order to do for ourselves. He is not a dictatorial God, but a God who wants us to discover the essence of who we are and live in harmony with that essence. This would be success—that we live the life meant for us and that is in harmony with God's will. He wants us to be successful in our lives and He sent Christ to teach us how to become strong, gain responsibility of self, and build our own world. In Christ's teachings and through His forgiveness, you will find the guidance in how to use and learn from adversity so that you can gain the inner strength to do anything—build your own world or change the big world around you. It is your choice. All you must do to start on *your* road to a successful and happy life is give your life to God and seek His guidance.

I bet that if the most intelligent man in the world lived on your street and he had the answers to all of your problems, you'd be there every day talking to him. Well, that person is right there inside you and He's talking to you through His word. If you can come up with one philosophy that Christ didn't cover, I'd like to hear about it. Christ really does have advice for every aspect of our lives and the Ten Commandments really do provide the truth and guidance we need to get our lives on track. Just remember that you cannot serve two masters—commit your life to God and reject the other distractions that try to take His place.

Most certainly you will make mistakes in life, but that's when you'll need repentance. Repentance is really just you reaching the stage of admitting and then accepting your mistakes. Once you do that, God helps you move forward again. The Bible tells me that the Triune God encompasses the three elements also found within us. The Father is spiritual—"God is a Spirit: and they that worship him must worship Him in spirit and in truth" (John 4:24). The Son is physical—"And the Word was made flesh, and dwelt among us…" (John 1:14). The Holy Spirit is mental, the part of us that is conscious and memory—"But the Comforter, which is the Holy Ghost, whom the Father will send in my name, He shall teach you all things, and bring all things to your remembrance, whatsoever I have said unto you (John 14:26). We too must put into harmony our spiritual, physical, and mental components. We need all three for a successful life and God's guidance can help us develop all three components of our life so that we are completely in balance. If either goes off balance—we make a mistake in thought, word or deeds—repentance helps us rebalance.

By God's grace we have hope. In faith, which is invisible faith, you can overcome all the adversity in your life and find your path to success. What I mean by invisible faith is that you must accept what you cannot see but can only feel. You must let go of doubt. We have all had those moments in life where something deep inside tells us to let go of the worry because everything will be okay. But then very often doubt creeps in. Stress and worry soon follow. That stress and worry can then cause us to make wrong decisions. The next time that God gives you that feeling deep inside that somehow all will be well, have faith and don't let the doubt creep in. Remember that faith really can move mountains. We really have no understanding of just how powerful our minds—a positive attitude—can be. We really only know a small amount about the mind, but we do know that we use only a small part of the human brain, and we have no conscious thought of how strong the mind is or of what it is capable. But I bet if you quiet your mind, you will begin to hear the internal guidance within you and you will discover how powerful your mental and spiritual components of your being can be.

The outline for a successful life is simple: remember that life is short and make the most of it.

#1 You have freedom of choice, so chose to:

Put the Triune God first.

Build your own world (handle adversity by remembering that everything earthly is temporary).

Accept and learn from adversity because it is the key to a successful life.

#2 Accept responsibility of self—you control your life, you are responsible for your decisions.

If you make a bad decision, ask for forgiveness.

And then *accept* that forgiveness and move on.

#3 Live your life doing what you love.

Find your passion in life.

If you make a wrong choice, learn from it.

Don't be afraid to act because you cannot fail (in every mistake there is a learning lesson).

#4 Remember that dreams grow, but wants fade:

Don't exchange your freedom for wants.

Needs are all that is important.

#5 Build wealth, don't make money.

The only value of money is to exchange it for what you want more than money.

If you build wealth, you build lives.

If you focus on making money, you just build monuments.

#6 Make a commitment to your life.

Commit to values and to truth.

Remember that illusions disappear under truths.

#7 Beware of deceit.

Separate wants from dreams.

The act is not the sin, the sin is the deceit of the act.

#8 Build your own world.

Seek God first.

Accept responsibility of self.

Let your dreams grow.

Do not deceive yourself.

When you make it to the top in life, remember this—the only thing you will find at the top is what you bring with you. Bring deceit, and that's what you will find up there. Bring truth and love with you, and that's what will be at the top. I want to close with a story I once heard: there is a man who spends his days sitting on his porch, looking down at a town in the valley. One day a car comes by and the people stop, sharing with the man that they just moved in to the valley town nearby. They ask him what kind of people live in that town, and he asks them what kind of people lived in the town they left. They tell him, "Oh, there were terrible people." The man says to them, "Well, that's the kind of people you'll find in that town down there." A little later another car comes by with people and they tell the man they just got transferred and are moving to the town down below. They ask the man, "What kind of people live in that town down there?" He asks them, "What kind of people live in the town you left?" They answer, "Oh, they were wonderful people. We'll really miss them." The man says, "Well, you'll find wonderful people in that town down there, too."

Bring Christ with you on your path to success and you will find not only success at the end of your path, but God, eternal love, peace, and happiness. If you have God, then you have love; and if you have that, you will always see the good in others and they the good in you. Human beings are images of God and God is a creator. If we are to fulfill our destiny as creators, then we must create and build our own worlds. The world that I have built for myself will end one day, and your world will end one day, too. But the world as a whole will go on as each individual builds his and her own world within the larger world. If each individual builds a world that is in glorification of the Triune God, imagine what the world as a whole can be. We are all connected to the infinite intelligence of the universe. Once you accept this, then you will realize that you have the power to build a world in which you will love to live. So get started.

LIMITS

Breeze so slightly, moves a slender blade of grass

Timeless matter, of no thought

Seas that end, never, only in our mind

Horizons end, by conscious thought

Illusions, of ourselves, timeless in their space

Known boundaries in self, limited by thought, conscious or not

A Spirit so slightly gives time without time, only truth

Boundaries need not be, being beyond time

Open timeless matter, to beyond self

Breeze so slightly, moves a slender blade of grass

– Carl Nafzger 2015

BIBLIOGRAPHY

Copenhaver, Jeff, *God Wants You to Win.*, The Master's Champions, 2009.

Frank, Anne. *The Diary of a Young Girl.* Random House Publishing, 1993.

Frankl, Viktor. *Man's Search for Meaning.* Beacon Press, 2006.

Hill, Napolean. *Think and Grow Rich.* Penguin Publishing Group, 2005.

Maltz, Maxwell. *Psycho-Cybernetics,* Pocket Books, 1989.

The Holy Bible. King James Version.

CPSIA information can be obtained
at www.ICGtesting.com
Printed in the USA
FFOW03n1616240417
34864FF